5 spices, 50 dishes

5 spices, 50 dishes

simple indian recipes using five common spices

by ruta kahate | photographs by susie cushner

CHRONICLE BOOKS

SAN FRANCISCO

For Ma and Tata,

my beloved parents, who introduced me to a world of excellent eating and cooking.

Library of Congress Cataloging-in-
Publication Data available.

ISBN-13: 978-0-8118-5342-2

Manufactured in China.

Designed by Benjamin Shaykin
Typeset in FF Clifford 9, MT Grotesque,
and H&FJ Numbers Indicia
Prop styling by Mary Ellen Weinrib
Food styling by Allison Attenborough

*The photographer wishes to thank the following
stores that loaned props: H Groome, Nine Main
St., Southampton, New York 11968, and 294
South County Rd., Palm Beach, Florida 33480;
Calvin Klein Home, Madison Avenue at 60 St.,
New York, New York 10021; Maya Schaper,
106 W. 69 Street, New York, New York 10023;
Paula Rubenstein, 65 Prince St., New York,
New York 10012; and Takashimaya New York,
693 Fifth Avenue, New York, New York 10022.*

10 9 8 7 6 5

Chronicle Books LLC
680 Second Street
San Francisco, California 94107

www.chroniclebooks.com

Acknowledgments

It all began with my parents, Gangadhar and Priyadarshini Kahate. Passionate about food, they'd constantly experiment and improvise in the kitchen, making meal times a joy. Seeking allies, they taught me and my brother, Yashodhar, how to cook when I was eleven, encouraging us through our early kitchen disasters. Without guidance from them and constant good-natured teasing from my brother, himself an excellent cook, I'd never have inherited their love and curiosity for all things culinary.

And without my husband Neville's support, I wouldn't have taken that passion and turned it into my profession. He urged me to pursue my hobby as a career and edited my recipes ruthlessly to the point where I could write them in my sleep. He'd hold our screaming baby for hours while I was teaching a cooking class and then help do the dishes after the class.

My kind, gentle mother-in-law, Vivianne deSouza, continues to be another huge culinary influence, sharing my ability to talk about food any time of day or night. Over the years, she taught me everything she knows about Goan cuisine, generously sharing her old family recipes.

This cookbook wouldn't be a reality without my dear friend Linda Carucci and my editor, Amy Treadwell. I first met Amy while teaching a cooking class at Linda's home school and we became friends over a shared interest—our children. Everyone should be lucky enough to get as kind and patient an editor.

And finally, twenty-five recipe testers all over the country and in the United Kingdom gave freely of their time and opinions, helping me decide which recipes made the cut. They were guided in this effort by my able assistant, Erin Wakida, who held the fort admirably while I was absent for several weeks leading my annual culinary tour in India.

Thank you all from the bottom of my heart.

table of contents

"you eat like this every day?"

I get asked this question all the time, usually by people with busy schedules or children. It's no use explaining that the meal was quite simple to make. "You're a chef," they scoff. "We're not." They have all these romantic notions of Indian cooking: complex sauces that take all day to cook, cupboards full of spices with unpronounceable names, secret techniques passed down from ancestors in a faraway land.

While Indian cuisine can be all of those things (my mother's signature *goda masala* contains forty-two ingredients, for instance), very few Indians cook that way on a daily basis—they have busy schedules and children, too. But I can understand my friends' disbelief. A weeknight meal quickly put together with a few spices can taste as if I'd slaved over it for hours.

That's the beauty of Indian cooking. You can create dishes that taste as though you put in a lot more ingredients and effort than you really did. All you need is a tiny bit of direction. And that's where this cookbook comes in.

My premise is simple: Using five common spices and a few easily available ingredients, you can make fifty superb, well-balanced Indian dishes. I've carefully chosen the spices for their aromatic properties and versatility. While the ingredients and steps are simple, you'll find the results are anything but.

Happy cooking, and may the Kitchen Gods be with you.

my promise to you

indian food that's not intimidating

To use this cookbook, you won't even have to step into an Indian store. The spices and ingredients are readily available at your local supermarket or health food store. The whole point is to keep everything simple and accessible enough that you'll be motivated to cook Indian as often as possible.

simple recipes, but not simplistic dishes

The recipes in this book don't require special equipment or hours of prep work, yet they'll yield some pretty spectacular dishes. My favorite party dish, Roasted Lamb with Burnt Onions (page 57), needs just two spices and a few short steps to create a flavorful, meltingly tender roast your guests will be talking about for days.

the same spices, but not the same flavors

Although you'll be using combinations of the same spices, every dish will have a unique flavor. Steamed Cauliflower with a Spicy Tomato Sauce (page 26) and Curried Mushrooms and Peas (page 34) share the same four spices, yet each dish tastes completely different.

rule #1: no hard-and-fast rules

Although I've provided sample menus (page 13) and serving suggestions, you won't need to limit yourself to these combinations. Feel free to serve non-Indian accompaniments with some of these dishes—I do, all the time. For instance, Anglo-Indian Beef Stir-Fry (page 51) goes really well with a green salad and French bread. If it feels right to you, that's really all that matters.

five simple spices

The following spices will allow you to make dozens of balanced, complex Indian dishes. They are common enough that you'll probably find them at your local supermarket. If not, look for them at a health food store.

1. coriander seeds add a lemony, earthy flavor that's best when the seeds are freshly ground. Coriander is the seed of the cilantro herb, and is one of the world's oldest known spices; traces of it have even been found in the tomb of Tutankhamen in Egypt. Used whole, coarsely crushed, or ground, coriander is an indispensable part of Indian cooking. Since it complements other spices so well, it finds its way into many of the Indian spice blends known as *garam masalas*.

2. cumin seeds have an aromatic, peppery flavor. Part of the parsley family, cumin was an important spice to the ancient Egyptians, Greeks, and Romans. It's certainly one of the most widely used spices in India, where it may have arrived via the armies of Alexander the Great. Indians cook with whole, ground, and roasted cumin. Aside from cooking, they like to chew cumin seeds after meals for digestive reasons.

3. mustard seeds are pungent, slightly bitter, and tiny. In fact, in ancient India, "one mustard seed" was the smallest weight on the scale. While mustard is used mostly as a prepared condiment in the West, Indians use the whole seeds in everything from simple dishes to complex curries, from spice blends to Indian-style pickles. Most Indian recipes use the black or brown variety, but in a pinch you can substitute the yellow kind.

4. ground cayenne adds heat, color, and a slightly smoky aroma. The cayenne pepper is one of the hotter varieties descended from *Capsicum annuum*, the original "chile" cultivated by the Aztecs thousands of years ago. Although India is the largest exporter of cayenne today, chile peppers were unknown in that country until the 1500s, when Portuguese sailors brought them from South America. In my recipes, "cayenne" refers to the red powder made from sun-dried red chile peppers of the same name. The "chili powder" sold in Indian stores can come from a variety of chiles and, as such, varies in color and level of heat.

5. ground turmeric adds a distinctive yellow hue and musky flavor that makes a lot of Indian dishes taste the way they do. Part of the ginger family, turmeric is a rhizome that has antibacterial properties, another reason Indians rub it on fish and meat—and on minor scrapes and burns. Handle turmeric powder carefully; it will transfer its signature yellow color to everything it touches, from your curries to your fingers.

the tabs on each recipe page show which spices are used in that recipe:

1. coriander seeds

2. cumin seeds

3. mustard seeds

4. ground cayenne

5. ground turmeric

one essential technique

Tadka is the basic Indian method for transferring the flavor from spices to food, and you'll use it over and over again. The name varies with the region of India—*tadka, bagar, chonkh, phodni*—but the technique is the same. First, the spices are added to very hot oil. The sizzling infusion or tadka is then used to flavor a dish. Here's how it works:

1. Heat the oil in a pan. Keep a spatter screen or lid handy—cumin and mustard seeds will sputter and pop wildly.

2. When the oil just begins to smoke, add the spice(s). Cover and allow the spice(s) to cook—this literally takes seconds. As soon as the sputtering stops, the tadka is ready.

3. Immediately add the larger ingredients to the pan—this cools the oil and prevents the spices from burning.

Since the oil has to be very hot, making a tadka takes a tiny bit of skill and speed. If you do burn the spices, don't panic. Discard them, rinse the skillet, and start over. Once you've done it a couple of times, you'll be an expert.

TIP #1: *Don't prepare a tadka in advance. Make it only when you're absolutely ready to use it, because it's most potent at the point when the spices are sizzling.*

TIP #2: *Since the tadka is ready in seconds, you won't have time to refer back to your recipe. So keep the ingredients for the next step on hand, ready to add to the pan.*

TIP #3: *A tadka may also be used to finish off a dish, by pouring it over a prepared raita or dal to impart a delicious smoky flavor. In this case, take it off the heat as soon as the spices stop sputtering and add it immediately to your dish.*

before you pick up that pan

Here are some general pointers that will help you make my recipes with predictably excellent results.

picking and using green chiles

Fresh green chiles are indispensable to Indian cooking because they add a type of heat and flavor that's different from the powdered red variety. My recipes use fresh green serrano chile peppers, which are available at most large supermarkets. If you need a substitute, look for any thin-skinned hot green chile, like *chile de arbol*, which is sold at Mexican markets. Avoid jalapeños—their skins are too thick for most Indian preparations.

The tricky part is judging the heat of the chile. The same kind of chile from the same market will vary in heat depending on the season and on how much sun the plant received. So please adjust the amount of fresh green chiles in my recipes to suit the particular chile you're using and your own tastes. One way to get the flavor (and vitamin C) of a green chile without the heat is to simply seed it. Cut the chile lengthwise and scrape out the seeds and fibers from inside each half. If you have sensitive skin or you're not used to working with chiles, be sure to wear rubber gloves or coat your hands with oil. And don't touch your eyes until you've washed off all the chile residue with soap and water.

making ginger and garlic pastes

Lots of Indian recipes call for fresh ginger and garlic crushed into fine pastes. A mortar and pestle is traditionally used, but a fine grater achieves comparable results with minimum time and effort. One of my favorite tools is a Japanese ginger grater—it costs all of $2 and reduces both ginger and garlic to a smooth, silky paste that's perfect in Indian recipes. A Microplane zester works well, too. Don't use a box grater, though; the holes aren't tiny enough, and it's a hassle trying to retrieve a teaspoon of paste from the awkward opening.

whole vs. ground spices

Although some of my recipes call for ground cumin and coriander, don't buy them that way. Buy the whole seeds instead, since you'll also be using them in other forms: whole, coarsely crushed, and roasted. Besides, store-bought ground spices quickly lose their flavor—often while sitting on the shelf. You'll get far better results if you buy one of those $15 coffee grinders and grind your spices to order. Just be sure to reserve the grinder for spices only—there's nothing worse than cumin-flavored coffee!

Some of my recipes call for roasted cumin and coriander. It's okay to roast and bottle small batches of these spices ahead of time. But again, grind them to order.

Exceptions to the rule: It's hard to find whole turmeric, so it's okay to buy this spice in ground form. Just buy the smallest quantity available and keep the container tightly sealed. Ground cayenne is fine too, for the simple reason that if you tried to grind red chiles, I'd be on your hit list as soon as you recovered from a violent sneezing fit.

cooking oil

Canola oil is used in most of my recipes. It has a high smoke point, which goes well with our tadka technique. I should mention that people in India use a variety of other oils as well: mustard in the north and east, untoasted sesame and peanut in the west, and coconut in the south. As my mother says, "Even the oil you use should have flavor." So if you do have a good peanut oil, by all means use it. The other oils—mustard, coconut, and sesame—tend to be pretty strong, so unless you're very familiar with regional Indian cooking, I would avoid them.

cilantro as a garnish

You'll notice that a lot of my recipes use minced cilantro as a garnish. Indians love this herb, and Indian recipes are well complemented by it. However, I'm sensitive to the fact that not everyone likes the taste of cilantro. If you're one of those people, feel free to exclude it from the recipe.

a few words about salt

I've used kosher salt for all the recipes in this book. But since people use different types of salt and have different levels of tolerance for it, please use my measurements only as a guideline. The crystals in kosher salt are large, so one tablespoon of kosher salt is roughly equal to half that of regular table salt. Used properly, salt helps bring out the flavor of food, so don't be afraid of it.

coconut milk

Coconut milk is traditionally made by steeping the grated flesh of fresh coconut in hot water and then squeezing it through cheesecloth to make the creamy liquid that tastes so exquisite in curries. The first press yields the "cream," and subsequent pressings result in thinner milks used to prepare lighter curries. This is quite a time-consuming process, so I am thankful coconut milk is available in cans now. But I must warn you, not all brands of canned coconut milk are good; some

are downright nasty. Good coconut milk tastes fresh, rich, and mildly sweet. A test is to check if the milk and cream separate inside the can. Artificially homogenized coconut milk has additives that keep the cream from naturally floating to the top. Also, do not use cans labeled "Cream of coconut" in my recipes; this is actually a sweetened, thicker product. Reserve it for your piña coladas. And one last word: Steer clear of "lite" coconut milk, as it has no substance or flavor.

a few menu ideas

are included here to get you started. You can use them as they are, or you can improvise with them—don't let them limit you in any way. Also, as I've mentioned earlier, there are no hard-and-fast rules. Steamed rice goes with just about everything on an Indian menu. And the sky won't fall on your head if you serve a curry without Indian flatbread. In fact, lots of Indians enjoy curry with a rustic bread, sometimes even with sliced white bread.

a last-minute meal
Anglo-Indian Beef Stir-Fry (page 51)
French bread
Tossed green salad

a weeknight supper
Onion and Yogurt Egg Curry (page 66)
Turkey and Basmati Rice Pilaf (page 106)
Spinach Raita with Toasted Cumin (page 95)
Fresh fruit salad with vanilla ice cream

a rainy night dinner
Butternut Squash and Green Beans in a Coconut-Milk Curry (page 28)
Store-bought mango or apricot chutney
Steamed rice

a summer bbq
Thalipeeth (page 107) with Roasted Onion Raita (page 98) as a dip
Lamb Chops with a Spicy Rub (page 54)
Spicy Seared Shrimp (page 75)
Tangy Shredded Cabbage Salad (page 90)
Corn with Mustard Seeds (page 32)
Black-Eyed Pea Salad with Ginger and Red Onion (page 87)

a sunday brunch
Masala Omelet (page 67)
Railway Potatoes (page 20)
Bread and butter
Fresh fruit
Ginger Chai (page 127)

a kids' menu
Mild Fish Stew with Potatoes (page 81)
Goan Savory Crêpes (page 113)
Cardamom Nankaties (page 122)

a girlfriends' lunch
Black-Eyed Peas in a Spicy Goan Curry (page 40)
Crispy Okra Raita (page 93)
Chapati (page 109)
Lemongrass Chai (page 127)

a seafood dinner for six
Shrimp Cakes with Ginger and Cilantro (page 76)
Watercress salad
Goan Shrimp Curry with Eggplant (page 71)
Indian Fried Fish (page 79)
Steamed white rice

a valentine's dinner for two
Mussels in a Green Curry (page 73) with French bread for dipping
Baked Fish in a Spice Broth (page 82)
Fresh green salad
Shrikhand with Yogurt Cheese, Saffron, and Pistachios (page 119)
Vanilla Bean Chai (page 127)

a buffet party
Vegetables with a Minty Lamb and Rice Stuffing (page 52)
Dal Poories (page 111)
Steamed Cauliflower with a Spicy Tomato Sauce (page 26)
Everyday Yellow Dal (page 39)
Crunchy Cucumber Salad with Crushed Peanuts (page 88)
Shrikhand with Yogurt Cheese, Saffron, and Pistachios (page 119)

an elegant dinner for four
Lamb Chops with a Spicy Rub (page 54)
Crusty Russet Potatoes with Coriander (page 23)
Curried Mushrooms and Peas (page 34)
Rava Tea Cake with Almond Paste and Rose Water (page 120)
Cardamom Chai (page 127)

a holiday spread
Chicken in Cashew Nut Sauce (page 65)
Roasted Lamb with Burnt Onions (page 57)
Sautéed Beets with Mustard and Lemon Juice (page 31)
Sweet Potatoes with Ginger and Lemon (page 24)
Black-Eyed Pea Salad with Ginger and Red Onion (page 87)
Creamy Pumpkin Kheer with Cashew Nuts (page 123)

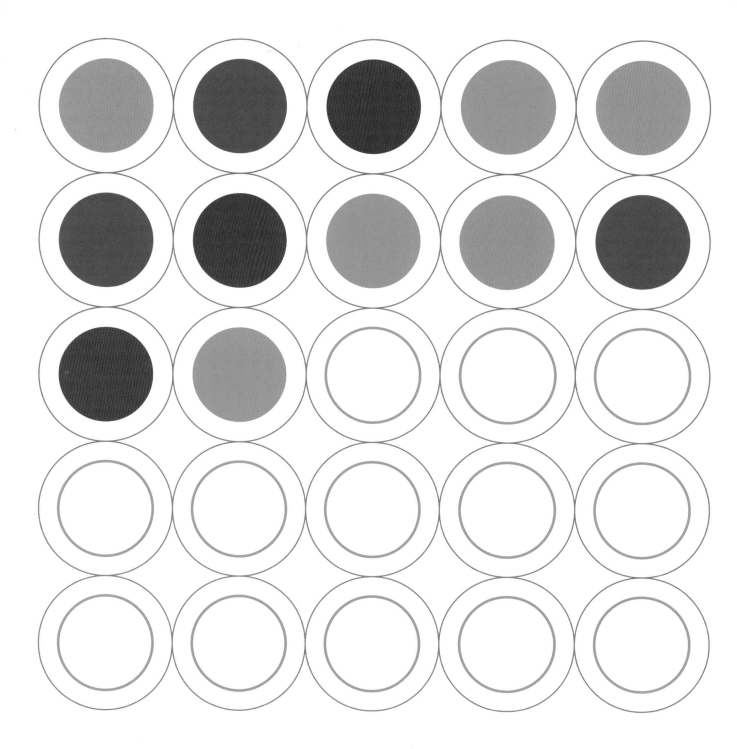

chapter **1:** vegetables

dishes **1–12**

"I don't miss the meat at all."

One of the highest compliments I've received came from an avowed and life-long carnivore: my husband. Convinced that vegetarians survived on things like boiled beans, he was delighted (and not a little surprised) to discover dishes like Eggplant Stuffed with a Sesame-Peanut Masala. With food like this, it's easy to be a vegetarian.

And with more than 70 percent of the world's vegetarians living in India, the breadth of its vegetarian cuisine is simply amazing. So although this section has just twelve recipes, I wanted to showcase as much variety as possible, from the wide range of produce to the way it's prepared—steamed, curried, sautéed, and stir-fried.

eggplant stuffed with
a sesame-peanut masala

This dish is perfect for entertaining. It looks stunning on a serving platter, yet it's exceptionally easy to put together—and can be made ahead of time. As a bonus, it can also be cooked in the oven, freeing up valuable burner space. The dish cooks faster and tastes better prepared the stovetop way, but you can decide what works best for you. I've made it for dinner parties as an entrée for my vegetarian guests but find that I often run out—thanks to the meat eaters at the table! Don't be daunted by the length of the recipe; it really is very simple to make.

¼ cup brown (natural) sesame seeds

½ cup raw or lightly toasted unsalted peanuts

⅓ cup cilantro leaves, finely chopped

2 tablespoons brown sugar

2 teaspoons salt

¼ cup plus 2 teaspoons water, divided

1 teaspoon finely grated garlic (about 2 large cloves)

½ teaspoon cayenne

½ teaspoon ground turmeric

8 mini Indian eggplants or 6 of the smallest Italian or Japanese eggplants you can find (about 1½ pounds)

¼ cup canola oil

Using a coffee grinder or food processor, separately pulse the sesame seeds and peanuts to semi-coarse powders. You don't want fine powders, but neither do you want chunks of peanuts in your filling. Remove to a bowl. Add the cilantro, sugar, salt, 2 teaspoons of the water, garlic, cayenne, and turmeric to the powdered mixture and mix well with your fingers. The mixture should become lumpy—if it doesn't, add a few more drops of water. Taste and adjust the salt and sugar if needed. The filling should taste slightly sweet and a little salty.

Leaving the stem end intact, make 2 intersecting diagonal cuts on the bottom end of each eggplant. You are basically making an "×." Do not cut all the way through. Be sure to leave the stems on. Stuff each × with the filling, packing it down well. This is easier said than done—it will feel awkward, but just push in as much filling as the eggplant will take, using your fingers to gently pry open the eggplant. Here is where you will thank yourself for having followed instructions to make the filling lumpy, since it sticks together better.

Heat the oil in a skillet large enough to hold all the eggplants in a single layer. Gently place each eggplant in the pan and turn the heat to medium. Turn the eggplants occasionally so they are evenly browned on all sides. Don't worry too much if some of the filling spills out. Once all the eggplants are browned, pour in the remaining ¼ cup water, cover, and cook on low until tender, about 15 minutes. To check doneness, pierce the stem end of each eggplant with

(continued)

a small, sharp knife—it should slide in easily. The whole eggplant should feel soft to the touch as well.

Instead of pan braising it, you may braise the eggplant in the oven: Use an ovenproof skillet. After browning the eggplant on the stovetop, pour in the water, cover, and transfer the skillet to a preheated 350°F oven and roast until the eggplant is tender, between 20 and 40 minutes, depending on the size of the eggplant.

This recipe can be made a day ahead. Simply reheat in a 375°F oven until warm.

Serves **4** to **6**

TIP: *One of my recipe testers in the U.K. came up with an ingenious variation. She couldn't find small eggplants, so she used a single globe eggplant instead, thinly sliced it lengthwise, and softened the slices a bit in hot oil. Then she stuffed each slice with the filling, rolled it up like a jelly roll, and secured it with a toothpick. She followed the rest of the recipe to finish the dish.*

spicy eggplant with tomatoes

This eggplant dish has been a hit in my classes ever since I began teaching Indian cooking. It's quite a spicy dish, but remember—you can always reduce the amount of cayenne. To create a complete North Indian vegetarian meal, serve with Chapati (page 109), Creamed Farmer Greens (page 35), and Punjabi Red Beans (page 43).

1 large Italian eggplant (about 1 pound)

3 tablespoons canola oil

1 medium onion, finely chopped (about 1½ cups)

1 teaspoon finely grated garlic (about 2 large cloves)

1 teaspoon finely grated fresh ginger (about 2-inch piece)

1 teaspoon ground turmeric

1 teaspoon cumin seeds, finely ground

1 teaspoon cayenne

2 medium tomatoes, finely chopped (about 1½ cups)

1½ teaspoons salt

1 teaspoon sugar

Cut the eggplant into ½-inch cubes.

Heat the oil in a large wok over medium heat and sauté the onion until softened, about 5 minutes. Add the garlic, ginger, turmeric, cumin, and cayenne, and sauté for another 2 minutes. If the mixture begins to stick to the bottom of the pan, deglaze by adding a few tablespoons of water and using a spatula to loosen the browned bits.

Add the eggplant, tomatoes, salt, and sugar, and toss until the eggplant is well coated with the onion-spice mixture. Cover and cook over medium-low heat until the eggplant is soft but not mushy, about 10 minutes. Serve warm.

Serves **4**

railway potatoes

My parents loved to travel, and they didn't let our school schedules get in the way. Every now and then, they'd pull us out of school for a few days and, much to our delight, we'd find ourselves on a cross-country train en route to our next family adventure. On those journeys, my mother would bring her signature "travel food"— these spicy, oniony potatoes, accompanied by buttery Chapatis (page 109). Even before the train pulled out of the station, my brother and I would be demanding she open the hamper!

1½ pounds medium red potatoes

5 tablespoons canola oil

½ teaspoon mustard seeds

¼ teaspoon ground turmeric

1 large yellow onion, halved and thinly sliced (about 2 cups)

2 teaspoons salt

¼ to ½ teaspoon cayenne

Slice the potatoes lengthwise into quarters. Then cut them crosswise into ⅛-inch-thick slices.

Make the tadka: Heat the oil in a large wok over high heat. When the oil begins to smoke, add the mustard seeds, covering the pan with a lid or spatter screen. After the seeds stop sputtering, add the turmeric and stir for a second. Immediately add the onion, potatoes, salt, and cayenne. Toss well, cover, and cook on medium heat until the potatoes are tender, tossing occasionally, about 10 minutes. Serve now or pack in an airtight container to take on a road trip.

Serves 4

a simple cabbage stir-fry

I clearly remember the first time I ate a version of this dish. I was six years old and couldn't tolerate spicy food at the time. But this cabbage stir-fry was so good, I ate as fast as I could, tears streaming down my face. I figured if I ate really fast I wouldn't feel the pain, and so I wouldn't have to stop eating. Don't worry—the recipe isn't that spicy; I just had a delicate palate as a child. I like my cabbage with some of the crunch left in it, but if you prefer, you can continue cooking until the cabbage is quite soft.

¼ cup canola oil

½ teaspoon mustard seeds

½ teaspoon ground turmeric

1 pound green cabbage, sliced
   very thinly

2 cloves peeled garlic, smashed
   with the side of your knife
   (optional)

1 teaspoon salt

½ teaspoon cayenne

Make the tadka: Heat the oil in a large wok over high heat. When the oil begins to smoke, add the mustard seeds, covering the wok with a lid or spatter screen. After the seeds stop sputtering, add the turmeric and sliced cabbage. Now add the garlic (if using), salt, and cayenne, and toss well.

Cover, reduce the heat to medium, and steam until the cabbage is crisp-tender, about 5 minutes. Serve hot.

Serves 4

crusty russet potatoes with coriander

Soft on the inside and crisp on the outside, these potatoes will go very well with your next pot roast or steak. You can also use them to add a subtle Indian touch at breakfast by serving them with buttery scrambled eggs.

4 large russet potatoes (about 2¼ pounds), boiled and peeled

6 tablespoons canola oil

½ teaspoon cumin seeds

2 medium green serrano chiles, cut lengthwise in quarters

1 teaspoon ground turmeric

1 teaspoon salt

3 tablespoons coriander seeds, coarsely crushed

Slice the potatoes lengthwise into quarters. Then cut them crosswise into 1-inch pieces.

Make the tadka: Heat the oil in a large wok over high heat. When the oil begins to smoke, add the cumin seeds, covering the pan with a lid or spatter screen. After the seeds stop sputtering, add the chiles. When the chiles are well toasted, add the turmeric and briefly stir. Add the potatoes and salt, toss well, cover, and leave on medium-high heat until the potatoes are slightly toasted, about 4 minutes.

Uncover and add the coriander seeds and toss well again. Continue to heat uncovered, tossing occasionally, until the potatoes are crusty and well browned, 6 to 8 minutes. Serve warm.

Serves 4

sweet potatoes with ginger and lemon

If you like sweet potatoes, you will absolutely love this dish. The ginger and lemon complement the sweetness of the vegetable. Serve with Dal Poories (page 111) for Sunday brunch.

2 pounds sweet potatoes and/or yams

2 tablespoons canola oil

½ teaspoon mustard seeds

2 small green serrano chiles, cut horizontally in half

1 medium red onion, finely chopped (about 1½ cups)

1 teaspoon finely grated fresh ginger (about 2-inch piece)

½ teaspoon ground turmeric

½ to ¾ teaspoon salt

2 tablespoons lemon juice, or to taste

Boil the sweet potatoes in water to cover until just tender. Cool, peel, and cut into 1-inch pieces.

Make the tadka: Heat the oil in a large sauté pan over high heat. When the oil begins to smoke, add the mustard seeds, covering the pan with a lid or spatter screen. When the seeds stop sputtering, add the chiles. When the chiles are toasted, add the onion and ginger. Sauté until the onion is lightly browned, then add the turmeric and stir.

Add the sweet potatoes and salt and toss gently to mix. Cover and steam over low heat until the flavors meld, about 4 minutes. Sprinkle the lemon juice over and serve hot or at room temperature.

Serves 4

steamed cauliflower with a spicy tomato sauce

My parents entertained often when I was a young child, and this dish would appear time and again on my mother's menus. It's easy to prepare, the presentation is quite impressive, and it's tasty as well—all necessary ingredients in a party dish.

2 small heads cauliflower (about 1 pound 12 ounces)

2 cups water

1 teaspoon salt, divided

½ teaspoon cumin seeds

1 teaspoon coriander seeds

3 tablespoons canola oil

1 teaspoon finely grated fresh ginger (about 2-inch piece)

1 teaspoon finely grated garlic (about 2 large cloves)

½ teaspoon ground turmeric

One 14.5-ounce can peeled, chopped tomatoes

1 medium green serrano chile, cut lengthwise in quarters

½ teaspoon cayenne

2 tablespoons minced cilantro leaves

Remove any leaves and cut off the tough stem parts of the cauliflower. Place the heads in a saucepan large enough to hold them comfortably, with the water and ½ teaspoon of the salt. Cover and simmer until the cauliflower is crisp-tender, about 10 minutes. If you like your cauliflower softer, by all means cook it longer. Set it aside and cover to keep warm while you make the sauce.

Roast the spices: Heat a small skillet over low heat and roast the cumin seeds until dark and fragrant. Remove the cumin from the pan and set aside to cool. Now add the coriander seeds and slowly roast them until dark brown. Be careful not to burn the spices. When the coriander seeds have also cooled, use a clean coffee grinder to grind them with the cumin seeds and set aside.

Heat the oil in a large saucepan and add the ginger, garlic, and turmeric. Stir constantly over medium heat until the mixture turns golden brown. This will happen quickly, so be careful it doesn't burn. Crush the tomatoes with your hands and add them to the pan along with all the juices. When the tomatoes come to a boil, stir in the chile, cayenne, cumin, coriander, and remaining ½ teaspoon salt. Lower the heat and simmer the sauce until the tomatoes are well cooked, about 8 minutes. You will be able to tell by the fact that the oil will start to separate from the sauce. Add the cilantro and simmer for another 1 to 2 minutes to heat through.

Place the warm whole cauliflower on a platter, pour the sauce over the top, and serve immediately.

Serves 4 to 6

butternut squash and green beans in a coconut-milk curry

This is a South Indian–inspired sweet, mild curry. Serve it with steamed white rice and a tangy fruit chutney like cranberry or mango for a perfect rainy day meal. The recipe calls for a rather small quantity of butternut squash, so you may want to reserve the rest of the squash for Butternut Squash Raita with Ground Mustard (page 96).

8 ounces butternut squash, peeled and chopped into 1-inch cubes (see page 96)

½ cup water

Salt

8 ounces green beans, trimmed and chopped into 1-inch pieces

1 cup canned coconut milk

2 tablespoons canola oil

¼ teaspoon mustard seeds

2 medium green serrano chiles, minced

3 tablespoons coarsely chopped cashews

Place the cubed squash in a medium saucepan with the water and a pinch of salt and bring to a boil over high heat. Lower the heat to medium, cover, and steam until the squash is tender, about 6 minutes. Remove the squash with a slotted spoon and then add the green beans to the pan. Repeat the process, topping up the water if needed.

Return the squash to the pan with the green beans and any remaining cooking liquid. Add the coconut milk and a little more salt if necessary. Bring to a boil and immediately turn the heat down to low. Simmer the curry, uncovered, until slightly thickened, about 8 minutes—don't allow the mixture to come to a rolling boil or it will curdle. Do not stir because the squash may start disintegrating; shake the pan if you need to mix the ingredients.

Transfer the curry to a serving dish.

Make the tadka: Heat the oil in a small skillet or butter warmer over high heat. When the oil begins to smoke, add the mustard seeds, covering the pan with a lid or spatter screen. After the mustard seeds stop sputtering, add the chiles and cashews and shake the pan over medium heat until the cashews are toasted and lightly browned. Pour this over the curry and serve.

Serves 4

sautéed beets with mustard and lemon juice

This recipe transforms the humble beet from a hearty root vegetable into a light, fresh-tasting dish you can serve all year-round. You may use all red beets, but it makes for an attractive dish if you get a mixture of different colors. I love serving these beets with Everyday Yellow Dal (page 39), steamed rice, and Crispy Okra Raita (page 93) for a simple weeknight meal.

2 pounds gold and red beets (about 8 medium or 16 baby beets)

3 tablespoons canola oil

½ teaspoon mustard seeds

2 small green serrano chiles, sliced into ¼-inch rounds

1 teaspoon salt

1 tablespoon lemon juice, or more to taste

2 tablespoons minced cilantro leaves

Scrub and rinse the beets well. Cover with water in a medium pot and bring to a boil. Lower the heat and cook, covered, until tender, 20 to 30 minutes, depending on the size of the beets. Use a paring knife to test for doneness; if it slides into the thickest part of the beet fairly easily, they are done. Drain, cool, peel, and then chop the beets into ½-inch cubes if using medium-sized beets. Quarter the baby beets.

Make the tadka: Heat the oil in a wok over high heat. When the oil begins to smoke, add the mustard seeds, covering the pan with a lid or spatter screen. When the seeds have stopped sputtering, add the chiles and give a quick stir. Quickly throw in the beets and salt. Toss, cover, and steam over low heat for 6 to 8 minutes to allow the flavors to blend.

Remove to a serving dish and toss with the lemon juice and cilantro. Serve warm or cold.

Serves 4

corn with mustard seeds

Corn in India is neither tender nor sweet, so it's usually cooked with salt and spices to bring out the flavor. This recipe from my home state of Maharashtra is one of my favorite side dishes. The traditional method involves grating the corn off the cob to increase the tenderness. I've found that the recipe is just as delicious with sweet corn, but I simply cut the kernels off the cob instead of grating them.

5 ears fresh or frozen (thawed) yellow corn

3 tablespoons canola oil

½ teaspoon mustard seeds

1 or 2 small green serrano chiles, sliced thinly into rounds

¼ teaspoon ground turmeric

Salt

1 tablespoon minced cilantro leaves

Slice the kernels off the corn cobs; you should have approximately 4 cups of corn.

Make the tadka: Heat the oil in a medium wok or sauté pan over high heat. When the oil begins to smoke, add the mustard seeds, covering the pan with a lid or spatter screen. After the seeds have stopped sputtering, add the chiles and stir until they are well toasted. Lower the heat to medium and add the turmeric, stir, and add the corn and salt to taste. Toss well, turn the heat to low, cover, and cook the corn until soft and tender, about 5 minutes.

Stir in the cilantro and serve warm or at room temperature.

Serves 4

curried mushrooms and peas

This typical Northern Indian–style curry is a hit with vegetarians and non-vegetarians alike and goes extremely well with Indian breads. Round out your next Indian takeout order of naan and tandoori chicken with this hearty curry. Fresh English peas work better here; they take a little bit of time to shell, but are worth the effort. If you can't find fresh peas, use frozen ones—just know that they will add a bit of sweetness to the dish.

1 pound white or brown button mushrooms

2 tablespoons canola oil

1 tablespoon unsalted butter

1 small red onion, finely chopped (about 1 cup)

1 teaspoon finely grated ginger (about 2-inch piece)

1 teaspoon finely grated garlic (about 2 large cloves)

1 teaspoon cumin seeds, finely ground

1 teaspoon coriander seeds, finely ground

½ teaspoon ground turmeric

½ teaspoon cayenne

¼ cup chopped tomato (about 1 small)

¼ cup finely chopped cilantro

1¼ cups shelled peas, preferably fresh

1 cup water

½ teaspoon salt

Cut the larger mushrooms into quarters, and the smaller ones in half.

Heat the oil and butter together in a large pan, and sauté the onion until dark brown. Add the ginger, garlic, cumin, coriander, turmeric, and cayenne, and stir constantly over medium heat until the mixture turns golden brown. This will happen quickly, so be careful it doesn't burn. Add the tomato and cilantro and sauté another minute.

If using frozen peas, rinse them under water to thaw them a little. Add the peas and mushrooms to the spice mixture, mix well, add the water and salt, and bring to a boil. Turn the heat down to a simmer, cover the pan, and cook until the mushrooms are tender, about 10 minutes. Serve hot.

Serves **4**

creamed farmer greens

Slow-cooked mustard greens are a popular peasant dish in the state of Punjab. My version uses beet greens and kale, but any combination of hearty, soft greens such as mustard or chard will work. (Avoid collard greens in this recipe; the flavor combination is not optimal, in my opinion.) With very mild heat from the ginger, this dish makes a nice substitute for traditional greens at the holiday table.

1 bunch beet greens (about 12 ounces)

1 bunch kale (about 12 ounces)

1½ cups water, divided

2 tablespoons canola oil

¼ teaspoon cumin seeds

2-inch piece fresh ginger, peeled and julienned (about 1 heaping teaspoon)

1 medium yellow onion, thinly sliced (about 1½ cups)

Salt

¼ cup heavy cream

Rinse the greens well and discard any tough stalks. Coarsely chop the leaves and tender stems and place them in a large stockpot with 1 cup of the water. Cover and cook over medium-high heat until the leaves are tender, 15 to 20 minutes. Drain.

Make the tadka: Heat the oil in a large saucepan over high heat. When the oil begins to smoke, add the cumin seeds, covering the pan with a lid or spatter screen. After the seeds have stopped sputtering, add the ginger and onion and sauté over medium heat until the onion is dark brown.

In a food processor, coarsely purée the onion mixture and greens together. Return to the saucepan with the remaining ½ cup water and salt to taste, and cook, covered, over low heat for 30 minutes, allowing the greens to soften in flavor. Stir in the cream and serve warm.

Serves **4**

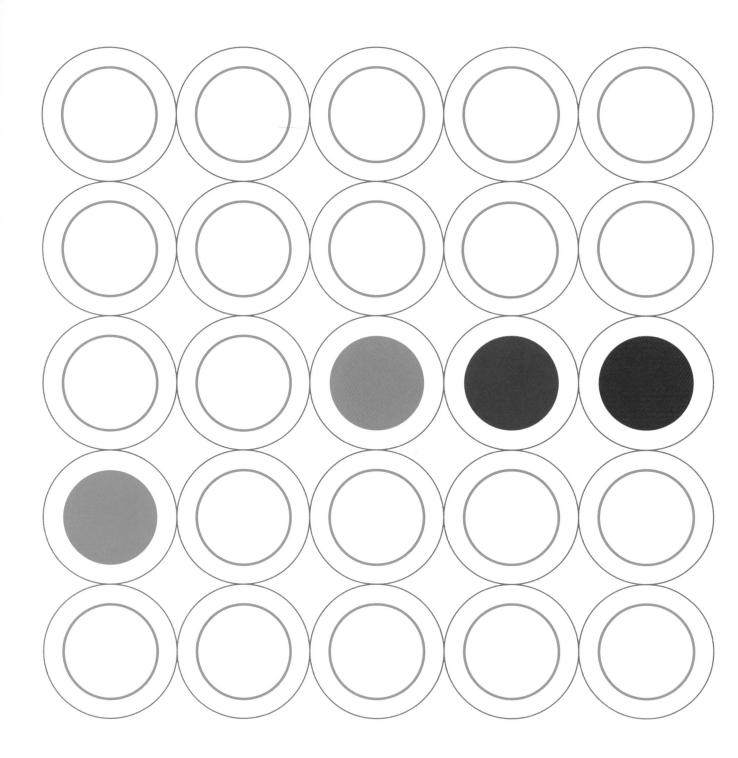

chapter **2:** dals

dishes **13–16**

Is *dal* a pulse, a legume, or a bean? Skinned or not? The raw ingredient or the cooked product? Soupy or thick? The term "dal" has confounded many a non-Indian cook. Even more confusing, the answer to those questions is: all of the above. "Dal" is a generic term for many kinds of pulses and beans—whole, split, skin-on, skin removed, and also the thick or thin cooked versions of them. There's even a "dry" cooked version!

But dal is even more than that. The combination called "dal rice" is the very essence of Indian cooking, and every region of the country has its own version. It's the main source of protein for vegetarians, yet non-vegetarians can't live without it. Cooked with rice into a gruel, it's one of the first solid foods given to infants. And when Indians need comfort, they turn to—you guessed it—a warming bowl of dal and rice.

In keeping with the spirit of my book, these recipes use dals that are easily found in a Western supermarket. Some of them even use canned versions that cut down on cooking and planning time without compromising on flavor.

everyday yellow dal

This simple dal goes with practically any Indian menu. It can be part of an elaborate meal, or simply ladled over freshly steamed rice with a little store-bought Indian pickle or chutney on the side. If you'd like to dress it up a bit, sprinkle a handful of Burnt Onions (page 58) on top just before serving.

1 cup yellow split peas, soaked in cold water for 1 hour

3 cups water

1 large tomato (about 8 ounces), cut into 8 wedges

¼ cup canola oil

½ teaspoon cumin seeds

1 medium red onion, finely chopped (about 1½ cups)

5 large cloves garlic, thinly sliced

1 teaspoon coriander seeds, finely ground

¾ teaspoon ground turmeric

½ teaspoon cayenne

¼ cup minced cilantro leaves

1 tablespoon unsalted butter

1 teaspoon salt

Drain the dal (split peas) and place in a large saucepan. Add the fresh water and tomato and bring to a boil. Reduce the heat to a simmer, cover, and cook until the peas are tender, 45 minutes to 1 hour. Pick out any tomato skins and whisk the dal to emulsify it. Keep warm over low heat.

Make the tadka: Heat the oil in a medium skillet over high heat. When the oil begins to smoke, add the cumin seeds, covering the pan with a lid or spatter screen. After the seeds have stopped sputtering, add the onion and garlic and sauté over medium heat until most of the onion has turned dark brown, about 5 minutes. Add the coriander, turmeric, and cayenne, stir, and pour the onion mixture over the dal. Add the cilantro, butter, and salt to the dal and simmer for another 5 minutes. Serve hot.

Serves 4

black-eyed peas in a spicy goan curry

My mother-in-law, who lives in a tiny village in Goa, serves these black-eyed peas piping hot for breakfast. On my visits there, I love to sit down to a steaming bowl with some freshly baked bread and listen to the sounds of the village waking up all around me—the baker making his morning rounds on his bicycle, the fishwomen bustling into the village square, and the children noisily arriving at the nearby school. You can serve this with Chapatis (page 109) or steamed rice, or simply on its own as a satisfying soup for lunch.

1 cup dried black-eyed peas or two 15-ounce cans, drained

2 tablespoons canola oil

1 small yellow onion, minced (about 1 cup)

1 teaspoon coriander seeds, finely ground

½ teaspoon finely grated garlic (about 1 large clove)

½ teaspoon finely grated fresh ginger (about 1-inch piece)

½ teaspoon ground turmeric

½ teaspoon cayenne

½ teaspoon cumin seeds, finely ground

¼ cup minced tomato (1 small tomato)

2 cups (or 1 cup if using canned peas) hot water

½ teaspoon salt, or to taste if using canned peas

½ teaspoon sugar

1 cup canned coconut milk

2 tablespoons minced cilantro leaves

1 tablespoon lemon juice

If using dried black-eyed peas, rinse and soak them in water to cover for 6 to 8 hours. Drain.

In a large saucepan, heat the oil over medium-low heat and sauté the onion until it turns dark brown, about 8 minutes. Add the coriander, garlic, ginger, turmeric, cayenne, and cumin, and stir for 2 minutes. Add the tomato and stir over low heat until it disintegrates.

Add the peas and mix well. Pour in the water, add the salt and sugar, and bring to a boil. Turn the heat down to low, cover, and simmer until the peas are cooked through, about 20 minutes. If using canned peas, simmer for only 10 minutes (it is essential to simmer the canned peas too, so that the flavors blend better). Stir in the coconut milk and simmer uncovered for another 8 to 10 minutes, again allowing the flavors to come together.

Add the cilantro and lemon juice, simmer for 1 minute more, and remove from the heat. Serve hot.

Serves 4 to 6

NOTE: *If you are using dried black-eyed peas, the cooking time can vary depending on the age of the beans.*

chickpea curry with fresh dill leaves

This recipe (see photo, page 2) traditionally uses a split and skinned Indian chickpea called chana dal, *but I've found that canned chickpeas work just as well—which makes it possible to create this dish in minutes. The other interesting thing is that it uses dill leaves in the typical Indian style—as a vegetable, rather than as an herb. Serve with Marathi Yellow Fried Rice (page 103) and Roasted Onion Raita (page 98) for a hearty vegetarian meal.*

2 tablespoons canola oil

1 medium yellow onion, finely chopped (about 1½ cups)

1 teaspoon cayenne (or less)

1 teaspoon coriander seeds, finely ground

1 teaspoon finely grated garlic (about 2 large cloves)

1 teaspoon finely grated fresh ginger (about 2-inch piece)

½ teaspoon ground turmeric

1 medium tomato, finely chopped (about 1 cup)

3 cups finely chopped dill leaves and tender stalks (about 2 bunches)

One 15.5-ounce can low-sodium chickpeas (garbanzo beans), drained

¼ cup water

1 teaspoon salt

Heat the oil in a medium saucepan and sauté the onion over medium heat until it has softened, about 5 minutes. Add the cayenne, coriander, garlic, ginger, and turmeric and stir for 3 to 4 minutes. Mix in the tomato and cook until it is soft, about 5 minutes. Add the dill, chickpeas, water, and salt, and simmer until the dill is soft and tender, 5 to 8 minutes. Serve warm.

Serves 4

punjabi red beans

This recipe is a staple in Punjabi households and is usually served with a more robust grain of rice than the delicate basmati—you can even use brown rice. Round off this satisfying meal with Fire-Roasted Eggplant Raita (page 94).

1½ cups dried red beans, soaked in cold water for 8 hours or overnight

4 cups water

3 tablespoons canola oil

1 medium yellow onion, finely chopped (about 1½ cups)

1 teaspoon finely grated garlic (about 2 large cloves)

1 teaspoon finely grated fresh ginger (about 2-inch piece)

½ teaspoon ground turmeric

One 14.5-ounce can peeled, diced tomatoes, puréed (about 1½ cups)

1 teaspoon coriander seeds, finely ground

½ teaspoon cumin seeds, finely ground

2 medium green serrano chiles, cut lengthwise in quarters

2 teaspoons salt, or to taste

Unsalted butter for garnish (optional)

Drain the beans and place in a large saucepan. Add the 4 cups water and bring to a boil. Reduce the heat to a simmer, cover, and cook until the beans are very soft, 1 hour or more.

Meanwhile, heat the oil in a medium skillet and sauté the onion until it is well browned. Add the garlic, ginger, and turmeric and stir for 2 to 3 minutes. Add the tomato purée, coriander, and cumin, and simmer until the sauce is thick. Stir this sauce into the pot of beans when they are tender, and add the chiles and salt.

Simmer, uncovered, for another 15 to 20 minutes to allow the flavors to come together well. Stir in the butter if using. This dish tastes best the day after it is made. Reheat gently over medium heat.

Serves 4 to 6

NOTE: *You may also use two drained 14-ounce cans of red beans here. Simply skip the first two steps.*

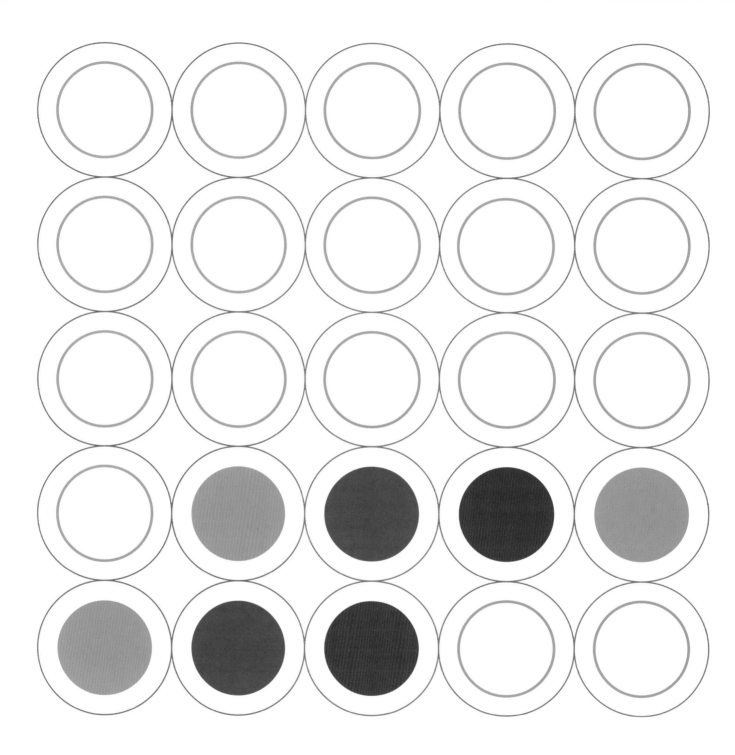

chapter **3:** beef and lamb

dishes **17–23**

Technically, my family isn't supposed to eat meat because they belong to the so-called Brahmin class. But my parents, unconventional as always, would cook delicious goat curries every Sunday. I was the only one at the table who abstained, driving everyone crazy with my lectures on animal rights.

Ironically, my love affair with meat began with the food most forbidden to me as a Hindu Brahmin: beef. Living on my own, I discovered the virtues of spaghetti with a good meat sauce. Then I married a man from Goa, possibly India's least vegetarian state. My mother-in-law introduced me to a new world of fabulous pork and beef preparations, like the Fried Green Beef I've featured in this section.

Even with all the taboos around red meat in India, it's prepared in a surprising variety of ways, not just in curries. That's because there are so many different communities that enjoy it, from Parsis to Anglo-Indians to Muslims. To reflect that breadth, here are some unique recipes. But if you're a curry lover, fear not: I have included two really good ones for you.

indian brown beef stew

This is what you would call an "everyday" meat curry in India. It's simple to put together, but you'll need to simmer the beef for about an hour until tender. Indians accomplish this in approximately one-third that time with a pressure cooker—an indispensable tool in every Indian kitchen. If you have a pressure cooker you inherited from Grandma, dust it off and put it to work; this curry would be ready in a mere twenty minutes. If you favor carrots over potatoes, feel free to substitute them.

3 tablespoons canola oil

1 large yellow onion, finely chopped (about 2 cups)

2 tablespoons coriander seeds, finely ground

2 teaspoons finely grated garlic (about 4 large cloves)

1 teaspoon finely grated fresh ginger (about 2-inch piece)

1 teaspoon cayenne

½ teaspoon ground turmeric

1 pound beef sirloin, cut into 1-inch square pieces

2 cups water

1½ teaspoons salt

2 large russet potatoes (about 1 pound), cut into 2-inch cubes

1 medium green serrano chile, cut lengthwise in quarters

1 tablespoon rice vinegar or apple cider vinegar

Heat the oil in a large stockpot and sauté the onion until golden. Add the coriander, garlic, ginger, cayenne, and turmeric, and stir over medium heat until browned, about 4 minutes. Deglaze the pan by adding a few tablespoons of water and using a spatula to loosen the browned bits, if the mixture starts sticking to the bottom.

Add the beef and sauté over medium heat until well browned, 5 to 10 minutes. Add the 2 cups water and salt and bring to a boil. Reduce the heat to a simmer and cook, covered, for 1 hour. Add the potatoes and chile and continue cooking until the beef and potatoes are tender, another 15 to 20 minutes.

Add the vinegar, simmer for an additional 2 minutes, and remove from the heat. Serve hot with crusty bread or steamed white rice.

Serves 4

fried green beef

DISH
18

My husband's all-time favorite dish, these thin beef cutlets are smeared with a spicy green paste and pan-fried. They're so good, it really is hard to stop at one. They're best eaten as they come out of the skillet, and my husband takes that seriously, leaving none for the actual dinner table. If you anticipate a similar problem in your kitchen, resign yourself to serving them as an appetizer!

2 pounds London broil (inside round)

2½ cups coarsely chopped, tightly packed, rinsed cilantro leaves and tender stems (about 1 bunch)

2 medium green serrano chiles, coarsely chopped

2½ tablespoons lemon juice

2 tablespoons water

1½ teaspoons finely grated fresh ginger (about 3-inch piece)

1 teaspoon finely grated garlic (about 2 large cloves)

1 teaspoon salt

¼ teaspoon ground turmeric

¼ teaspoon cumin seeds, finely ground

½ cup or more canola oil

1 cup rava, semolina, or cream of wheat (not the quick-cooking kind) (see Note)

Ask your butcher to slice the meat into ½-inch-thick slices. When you get home, lay the slices between sheets of plastic wrap and pound with a mallet until each slice is about ⅛ inch thick. These slices are huge, so I usually cut each pounded scaloppine widthwise into 2 pieces. You will end up with 10 to 12 slices.

Using a food processor or blender, grind the cilantro, chiles, lemon juice, water, ginger, garlic, salt, turmeric, and cumin to a smooth, fine paste. Taste for seasoning and adjust the lemon juice and salt as needed; the masala should taste slightly tart as well as salty. Smear the masala over the meat, turning and restacking each piece to ensure that all the slices are evenly covered. Set aside to marinate for 30 minutes or up to 12 hours in the refrigerator.

Heat the oil in a large, heavy skillet. Place the rava in a large bowl or plate. Remove any big gobs of marinade from the scaloppine but don't scrape all the marinade off; you want as much of it to stay on as possible. Dip each scaloppine in the rava and dust well on both sides. Pan-fry in batches until crisp and browned, 3 to 4 minutes on each side. Do not overcrowd the pan. Remove to a paper towel–lined plate. Serve immediately.

Serves **4**

NOTE: *Rava, also called* sooji, *is Indian cream of wheat. It is available as both fine and coarse flours. You may use either.*

anglo-indian beef stir-fry

The British, Dutch, French, and Portuguese all colonized parts of India. This mingling of cultures trickled down to their tables, and today's Anglo-Indian is totally comfortable serving roasts, stews, and pies (all influenced by local ingredients and spices) alongside dal, biryani, and chapati. Perhaps the most well-known Anglo-Indian dish is Mulligatawny soup, but this easy stir-fry is also a popular one. The recipe evolved as a way to make use of a leftover roast, so if you have some, feel free to substitute it here.

1 pound beef sirloin or any other tender cut of beef, sliced against the grain into paper-thin slices

1 tablespoon rice vinegar or apple cider vinegar

1¼ teaspoons salt, divided

¾ teaspoon ground turmeric, divided

2 medium russet potatoes

6 tablespoons canola oil, divided

1 medium yellow onion, halved and thinly sliced (about 1½ cups)

1½ tablespoons minced fresh ginger (about 3-inch piece)

¼ teaspoon cayenne

To make slicing the beef easier, freeze it for about 20 minutes. Or even better, have the butcher slice it for you at the store. Rub the beef slices with the vinegar, 1 teaspoon of the salt, and ½ teaspoon of the turmeric and set aside.

Bring the whole potatoes to a boil in lightly salted water to cover. Boil them for 5 minutes, then turn off the heat, cover, and let the potatoes sit in the hot water for 10 minutes. The potatoes will be perfectly cooked without being mushy. Drain, peel, and cut into 6 to 8 wedges each. Coat the wedges with the remaining ¼ teaspoon turmeric and ¼ teaspoon salt. Set aside.

Heat 3 tablespoons of the oil in a large wok and fry the onion and ginger until softened slightly. Add the cayenne and then the marinated beef. Stir-fry over high heat until tender, 5 to 8 minutes. Cooking time will vary depending on which cut of beef you've used and how thinly you've sliced it. If you find that the beef is not tender enough for your liking, add ½ cup water, cover, and cook on medium-low heat until the beef is very tender, about 15 minutes more.

Meanwhile, heat the remaining 3 tablespoons of oil in a large skillet and gently fry the potato wedges over low heat until golden brown and crisp. Serve the stir-fry garnished with the potato "chips." By the way, a true Anglo-Indian would serve tomato ketchup alongside!

Serves **4**

vegetables with a minty lamb and rice stuffing

You may pick up Middle Eastern flavors in this mildly spiced recipe; I first tasted a version of it at a Jewish-Indian friend's home in Calcutta. Like my friend, you can choose a single vegetable to stuff, but I prefer a mélange because each vegetable makes the filling taste subtly different—and it's very attractive on a serving platter. You can stuff the vegetables up to four hours ahead of time and keep them refrigerated until ready to bake. Just remember to bring the vegetables to room temperature before placing them in the oven.

stuffing

½ cup basmati rice, soaked in water for 1 hour

8 ounces lean ground lamb

2 tablespoons minced mint leaves

1 tablespoon minced cilantro leaves

1 tablespoon lime juice

1 teaspoon finely grated garlic (about 2 large cloves)

1 teaspoon finely grated fresh ginger (about 2-inch piece)

1½ teaspoons salt

1 teaspoon canola oil

1 teaspoon sugar

½ teaspoon ground turmeric

½ teaspoon cumin seeds, finely ground

vegetables

1 large green zucchini

2 small, firm, slightly unripe tomatoes

2 small red bell peppers

2 small Indian, Italian, or Japanese eggplants

dressing

½ cup water

2 tablespoons canola oil

2 tablespoons lime juice

1 teaspoon sugar

½ teaspoon salt

Preheat the oven to 400°F.

Make the stuffing: Drain the rice and mix it with the lamb, mint, cilantro, lime juice, garlic, ginger, salt, oil, sugar, turmeric, and cumin. Use your fingers to break up the lamb and thoroughly mix everything together.

Prepare the vegetables: All the vegetables should be at room temperature. Slice off the ends and cut the zucchini horizontally into pieces about 3 inches long. With a thin, sharp paring knife, carefully core each piece all the way through, making a thin-walled, hollow pipe. Carefully take the tops off the tomatoes and bell peppers. Discard the seeds and pulp from the tomatoes. Cut out the seeds and white membrane from the peppers. Retain the stems of the eggplant and make an "✕" on the bottom end of each by cutting 2 lengthwise intersecting lines without slicing all the way through to the stem end.

Make the dressing: Whisk together the water, oil, lime juice, sugar, and salt.

Carefully stuff each vegetable only ¾ full with the stuffing, as the rice will expand when cooked. Place the vegetables in a single layer in a large, lightly oiled baking dish. Drizzle the dressing evenly over the vegetables, taking care to see that an inordinate amount doesn't fall into the tomatoes and bell peppers. Cover the dish with a lid or aluminum foil and bake, covered, until the rice and vegetables are tender, about 1 hour. Uncover the dish and place it under the broiler for a few minutes to brown just the edges of the vegetables. Serve warm.

Serves 4 to 6

lamb chops with a spicy rub

You have two hours before your guests arrive. You want to make something spectacular, but you're starting from scratch. Don't panic! It takes minutes to make this simple marinade. Rub it on the chops and set them aside, ready to be grilled just before serving time. Add a salad, mashed potatoes, or Crusty Russet Potatoes with Coriander (page 23), and you'll have an elegant meal. Then go arrange the flowers or sit down with a glass of wine, happy in the knowledge that your dinner guests will be properly impressed.

1 teaspoon finely grated fresh ginger (about 2-inch piece)

1 teaspoon finely grated garlic (about 2 large cloves)

¾ teaspoon salt

½ teaspoon cayenne

½ teaspoon cumin seeds, finely ground

½ teaspoon coriander seeds, finely ground

¼ teaspoon ground turmeric

8 lamb rib chops (about 1 pound 4 ounces)

3 tablespoons canola oil

In a bowl large enough to hold the chops, mix together the ginger, garlic, salt, cayenne, cumin, coriander, and turmeric to form a thick, slightly dry paste. Rub the chops well with this mixture and set aside to marinate for at least 2 hours and up to 8 hours in the refrigerator.

Heat a large cast-iron skillet over medium-high heat and add the oil. Sear the lamb chops to the desired doneness, 4 to 5 minutes on each side for rare. You may also grill these chops on an outdoor BBQ grill over high heat. Let rest briefly before serving.

Serves 4

roasted lamb with burnt onions

Could this dish really be so easy? It is, and I pinch myself every time I make it. The lamb, cooked in milk with almonds and raisins, has become a holiday staple in my home. I marinate the lamb the previous night and place the dish in the oven an hour before the guests arrive. The aromas filling the house are enough to infuse anyone with holiday spirit. By the way, the onions here are not actually burnt, but caramelized until crisp and dark brown, adding a rich sweetness to the lamb. Serve with chapatis as pictured.

¼ cup thick, plain, whole-milk yogurt

2 medium green serrano chiles, cut lengthwise in quarters

1½ teaspoons finely grated fresh ginger (about 3-inch piece)

1½ teaspoons finely grated garlic (about 3 large cloves)

1 teaspoon salt

½ teaspoon ground turmeric

½ teaspoon cayenne

1½ pounds leg of lamb, cut into 1½-inch pieces

1 recipe Burnt Onions (page 58)

2 tablespoons unsalted butter

3 tablespoons coarsely chopped almonds

3 tablespoons raisins

1 cup whole or low-fat milk

1½ tablespoons sugar

In a large bowl, mix together the yogurt, chiles, ginger, garlic, salt, turmeric, and cayenne. Taste and adjust the salt if necessary. Add the lamb and coat well with the marinade; set aside in the refrigerator for at least 4 hours and up to 12 hours.

While the lamb is marinating, make the Burnt Onions. If not cooking the lamb right away, refrigerate the drained and now crisp onions in an airtight container until ready to use.

Remove the lamb from the refrigerator at least 1 hour before roasting. Preheat the oven to 400°F.

Crumble the onions into the bowl with the lamb. Melt the butter in a skillet over low heat and separately toast the almonds until golden brown and the raisins until plumped, then set them on paper towels to drain. Scrape the butter into the marinating lamb. Pour the milk onto the lamb, add the sugar, and mix thoroughly.

Transfer the entire lamb mixture to a baking dish large enough to hold the lamb in a single layer. Cover tightly with a lid or foil and place in the middle of the oven. Roast, covered, for 1½ hours. The lamb will be cooked but not falling-apart tender, and the sauce will be thin. Uncover and continue roasting until the lamb is meltingly tender and the sauce has thickened, another 30 minutes.

Garnish with the almonds and raisins and serve.

Serves 4

burnt onions

These onions are fried until crisp and dark brown in color. You can use them as a delicious topping for many dishes, including Roasted Lamb (page 57). I like to serve them over pork chops or as a crispy topping for mashed potatoes. You can dress up Everyday Yellow Dal (page 39) or any of the pilafs in this book with a handful of burnt onions. Even plain steamed rice becomes special when garnished with them. I'm sure you'll dream up many more uses, so make a double batch and keep the rest refrigerated for up to one week in an airtight container.

1 large or 2 medium yellow
   onions

½ cup canola oil

Halve the onion(s) lengthwise and slice very thinly. Using your fingers, separate all the layers so you have individual half rings of onion. Heat the oil in a large skillet over high heat. Add the onions and stir until thoroughly coated with oil. Stop stirring and leave the skillet on high heat. The onions on the periphery will start to brown first. Stir them into the center of the pan, spreading the onions out again into an even layer. Do this occasionally until all the onions begin to color. Resist the urge to stir constantly.

Now lower the heat to medium-low and cook until all the moisture has left the onions, about 20 minutes. Stir occasionally. The onions should turn a very dark brown without actually getting burnt. When all the onions are evenly browned and crisp, drain on paper towels. They will crisp further as they cool. If you are not going to use them right away, store in the refrigerator in a tightly sealed container.

Makes approximately **2** cups

lamb meatballs in a spicy malabari curry

This spicy lamb dish from the Malabar coast of Kerala in South India is a quintessential "dipping" curry. Thin in consistency, it's perfect for soaking up with rustic bread or, even better, Goan Savory Crêpes (page 113). It's also delicious served over steamed rice. Like most coconut-milk curries, it tastes even better the next day.

meatballs

1 pound ground lamb

¼ cup minced shallots (about 1 medium shallot)

2 medium green serrano chiles, minced

1 teaspoon finely grated fresh ginger (about 2-inch piece)

¾ teaspoon salt

curry

2 teaspoons coriander seeds

1 teaspoon cumin seeds

3 tablespoons canola oil

½ teaspoon mustard seeds

4 shallots, halved and thinly sliced (about 1¼ cups)

5 cloves garlic, minced

1 tablespoon peeled, minced fresh ginger (about 1-inch piece)

½ teaspoon cayenne

⅓ cup tomato purée (from 1 small tomato)

One 14-ounce can coconut milk

½ cup water

2 medium green serrano chiles, cut lengthwise in half and seeded

1½ teaspoons salt

2 tablespoons minced cilantro leaves

1 teaspoon apple cider vinegar

To make the meatballs: Using your hands, mix the lamb with the shallots, chiles, ginger, and salt. Don't handle the mixture more than necessary, to ensure tender meatballs. Form about 20 golf ball–sized meatballs. Set aside.

To make the curry: In a dry skillet, separately roast the coriander and cumin seeds until lightly browned and fragrant. Cool and grind them together.

Heat the oil in a large saucepan over high heat. When the oil begins to smoke, add the mustard seeds, covering the pan with a lid or spatter screen. When the seeds stop popping, add the shallots, garlic, and ginger and stir constantly over medium heat, until the shallots turn golden brown. Add the coriander, cumin, cayenne, and tomato purée. Simmer for 5 minutes.

Add the coconut milk, water, chiles, and salt and bring to a boil. Immediately reduce heat to a simmer and gently slip in the meatballs. Continue simmering until the meatballs are cooked through, 8 to 10 minutes.

Add the cilantro and vinegar and shake the pan instead of stirring so you don't break the meatballs. Simmer gently for an additional minute. Serve hot.

Serves 4 to 6

NOTE: *If you prefer thicker curries, simply omit the water in the recipe.*

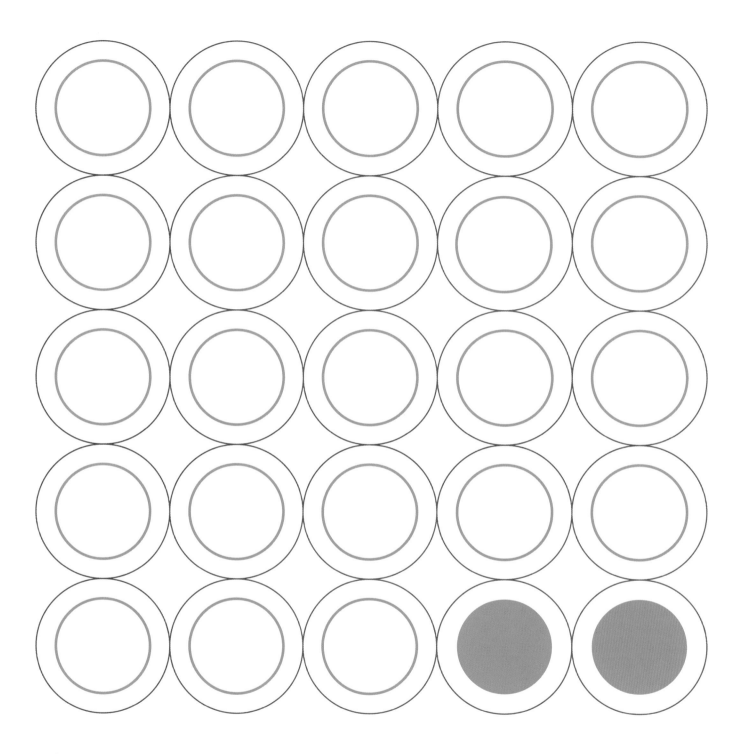

chapter **4:** chicken and eggs

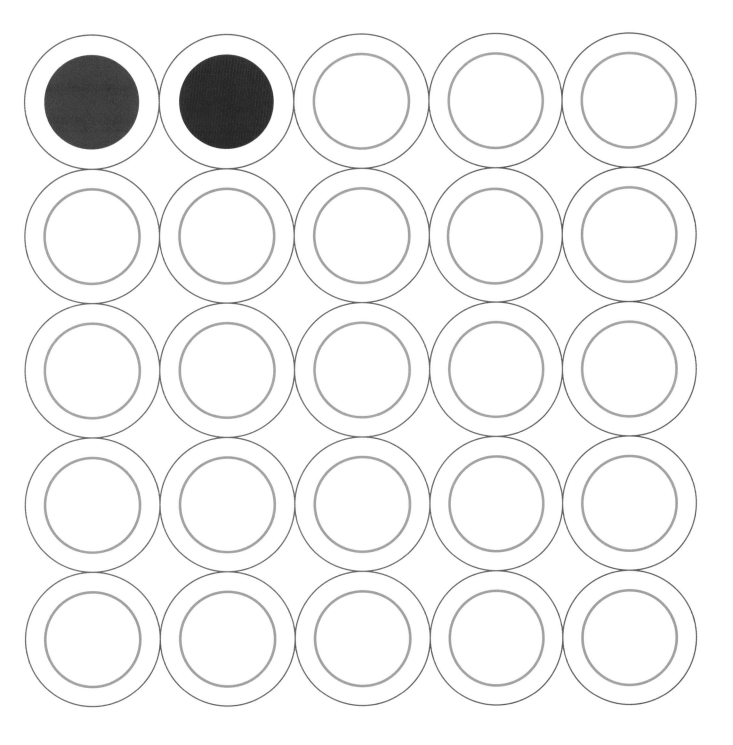

dishes **24–27**

When I was growing up in India, you either got your chicken from the local poultry vendor or had a few running around in the backyard. Cooking them took some effort; first you had to buy (or chase after and catch) the live bird. Then you had to butcher and dress it. Then came the endless simmering to loosen up tough muscles.

This reminds me of my mother-in-law's first chicken curry. A month after her wedding, her husband brought home a live chicken and the news that he'd invited his boss to dinner that night. She was very young, and didn't know how to cook, let alone butcher, anything. But after the tears had subsided, they did what needed to be done, following instructions dictated over the phone by an aunt. The chicken was served, the boss was impressed, but my mother-in-law couldn't eat a bite! That recipe, New Bride Chicken Curry, is featured at right.

Eggs are enjoyed as a main course in India, not just for breakfast. Even some vegetarians eat eggs; they're known as "eggitarians." Eggs are hard-boiled and curried, pan roasted with a dry mix of browned onions and spices, and whisked into spicy omelets with ginger, garlic, or fresh coconut. They're served with chapatis, steamed rice, and, yes, sliced white bread.

new bride chicken curry

This is the famous red chicken curry that my mother-in-law, Vivianne, cooked as a newlywed, after having to butcher and dress her very first live chicken (the only way you could buy a chicken at the time). I'm happy to report that she can now eat this curry without squirming at the memory of the first time she prepared it. Serve with some good French bread and Tangy Shredded Cabbage Salad (page 90).

4 tablespoons canola oil

2 medium yellow onions, finely chopped (about 3 cups)

2 teaspoons finely grated garlic (about 4 large cloves)

1½ teaspoons cayenne

½ teaspoon ground turmeric

¼ teaspoon cumin seeds, finely ground

1 cup plus 1 tablespoon hot water, divided

3 medium tomatoes, minced (2 cups)

3 pounds chicken parts (a combination of bone-in thighs and drumsticks works well here)

1½ teaspoons salt

1 tablespoon apple cider vinegar

1 teaspoon sugar

Heat the oil in a large pan over medium-high heat and sauté the onions until they turn dark brown. Mix the garlic, cayenne, turmeric, and cumin with 1 tablespoon of the water to make a thick paste. Add to the browned onions and sauté for 5 minutes. Add the tomatoes and stir constantly over medium heat until the tomatoes start to break up, about 2 minutes, making sure the mixture doesn't scorch.

Add the chicken and mix to coat with the spice paste. Stir over medium heat for 10 minutes. Add the remaining 1 cup water and the salt and bring to a boil. Lower the heat and simmer, uncovered, until the chicken is cooked through, about 30 minutes. Add the vinegar and sugar, simmer for 1 minute, and then taste. Adjust the salt, sugar, and vinegar if needed. This curry should be sweet and sour and spicy-hot. Serve hot.

Serves 4 to 6

chicken in cashew nut sauce

This recipe may challenge your perception of Indian food—it's neither spicy nor a curry. Using a technique borrowed from the old princely kitchens of North India, you'll use cashews to make a sauce that's surprisingly complex, despite its minimal ingredients. While most Indian chicken recipes call for bone-in meat, this sauce complements boneless chicken breasts very well. Serve with Lentil-Rice Pilaf (page 105).

3 tablespoons canola oil, divided

1 large yellow onion, thinly sliced (about 2 cups)

¾ cup water, divided

4 ounces finely ground raw unsalted cashews

1 teaspoon finely grated fresh ginger (about 2-inch piece)

1 teaspoon finely grated garlic (about 2 large cloves)

½ teaspoon cayenne

1 tablespoon unsalted butter

1½ teaspoons salt

4 skinless, boneless chicken breasts (about 1½ pounds), tenderloins removed

½ cup plain whole or low-fat yogurt, whisked

Heat 2 tablespoons of the oil in a medium skillet and fry the onion until well browned. Cool slightly and then use a food processor to grind the browned onion with ¼ cup of the water, the cashews, ginger, garlic, and cayenne until it forms a smooth, thick paste.

In a large saucepan, heat the remaining 1 tablespoon oil along with the butter. Add the cashew-onion paste and stir constantly over medium heat, deglazing the pan by adding a few tablespoons of water and using a spatula to loosen the browned bits until the sauce has browned evenly. This should take about 5 minutes.

Thin out the sauce with the remaining ½ cup water and stir in the salt. Add the chicken and turn to coat well with the sauce. Simmer, covered, over low heat until the chicken is cooked through but is not overdone, 8 to 10 minutes. You can discreetly pierce the thickest part of a breast with a paring knife and check for doneness. Carefully turn the chicken breasts over once during cooking. Turn off the heat.

Remove the chicken breasts to a serving platter, gently stir the yogurt into the sauce, and mix well. Immediately pour the sauce over the chicken and serve. If the dish has to sit for a while, return the chicken breasts to the pan after you have stirred in the yogurt, and cover to keep warm.

Serves 4

onion and yogurt egg curry

This curry is interesting for two reasons: The protein is in the form of hard-boiled eggs, and the curry itself is based on yogurt, which makes it light, tangy, and perfect for soaking up with a rustic white bread. I usually make this dish when I am pressed for time yet hankering for a curry. It doesn't take more than twenty minutes to put together and delivers all the satisfaction of a nice, meaty curry.

4 tablespoons canola oil, divided

1 medium yellow onion, finely chopped (about 1½ cups)

2 teaspoons coriander seeds, finely ground

1 teaspoon finely grated fresh ginger (about 2-inch piece)

1 teaspoon finely grated garlic (about 2 large cloves)

1 teaspoon cumin seeds, finely ground

1 teaspoon ground turmeric

1 teaspoon cayenne

1 cup plain whole or low-fat yogurt, whisked

1 cup water

½ teaspoon salt

¼ teaspoon sugar

8 large eggs, hard boiled

Heat 3 tablespoons of the oil in a large pan over medium heat and sauté the onion until it turns very dark brown. Add the coriander, ginger, garlic, cumin, turmeric, and cayenne, and stir constantly over medium heat until the mixture turns golden brown, about 3 minutes. This will happen quickly, so be careful it doesn't burn. Whisking constantly, add the yogurt to the onion mixture. Turn the heat down to low and simmer until the yogurt thickens and the oil separates and begins to float on top. Add the water, salt, and sugar and bring to a boil again, then turn the heat down to a simmer.

Meanwhile cut the eggs lengthwise into halves. Heat a medium skillet over medium heat, add the remaining tablespoon of oil, and place the eggs, cut sides down, in the pan. When they brown slightly, turn them over and repeat on the other side. (I do this to seal the yolks in so they don't fall out into the curry later.)

Add the browned eggs to the curry sauce and simmer for an additional minute to heat through. Serve immediately.

Serves **4**

masala omelet

These omelets are served any time of day or night. They are a popular street food and a specialty at Bombay's old Irani cafés, where they are served with the cafés' trademark buttered buns. Indians also serve these omelets with rice for an easy lunch. Best eaten right out of the skillet, this recipe can also be used to make very thin omelets that are then used to prepare sandwiches.

8 large eggs

½ cup minced shallots (about 2 medium shallots)

¼ cup minced tomatoes (about 1 small tomato)

3 tablespoons minced cilantro leaves

2 small green serrano chiles, minced

2 small cloves garlic, minced

½ teaspoon salt

Pinch of ground turmeric

8 tablespoons canola oil, divided

In a large bowl, whisk the eggs. Add the shallots, tomatoes, cilantro, chiles, garlic, salt, and turmeric, and mix well.

Heat 2 tablespoons of the oil in a medium skillet, preferably cast iron, over high heat. Pour in ¼ of the egg mixture, turn the heat down to medium, and cover the pan. Check after 2 minutes; if the bottom of the omelet is set, flip it over. Brown on the other side, uncovered, over medium heat. Indian omelets are best when browned. This is tricky to achieve without overcooking the eggs—that's why the omelets are made quickly over medium to high heat. Repeat until you have made the other 3 omelets. Serve immediately with tomato ketchup, an essential accompaniment to Masala Omelets.

To make thin omelets for sandwiches: Follow the instructions above but use just enough of the egg mixture to make each omelet only ⅛ inch thick. A thin omelet can be allowed to cool to room temperature. Butter 2 slices of good sandwich bread generously with salted butter (preferably a European butter), and then fold an omelet in to fit within the bread.

Serves **4**

chapter **5:** seafood

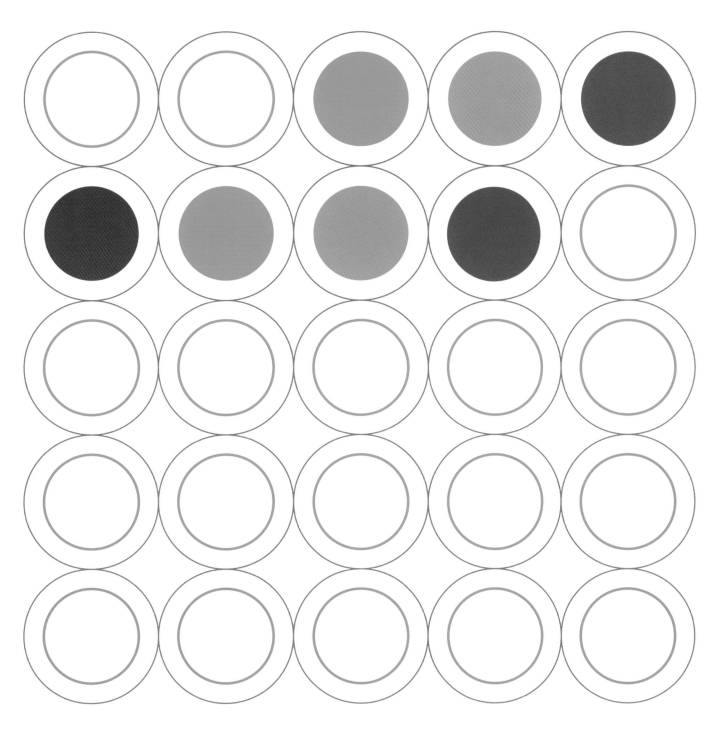

dishes **28–34**

A visit to a fishmarket in India is always an adventure. The men may bring in the catch, but it's the feisty women who rule the place. Brightly dressed and with flowers in her hair to offset the fishy odor, the fishwoman is a worthy opponent in the bargaining game you must play here. You may have been her loyal customer for years—but you're still very much expected to haggle.

Indian seafood dishes can be just as exciting, from mustard-infused fish-head curries in Bengal, to Portuguese-influenced salt cod in Goa, to fish steamed in banana leaves by the Parsi community. While exploring that kind of breadth is beyond the scope of this cookbook, I've tried to give you a small peek into it. With the exception of Shrimp Cakes with Ginger and Cilantro (page 76), any of these recipes can be made on a weeknight.

goan shrimp curry with eggplant

All along the western coast of Goa, you'll find picturesque fishing villages, ancient forts, golden beaches, and some of the most delicious seafood in the country. The fruit of the ubiquitous coconut palm finds its way into many local shrimp curries, along with an array of vegetables—summer squash, okra, green mango, and, my very favorite, eggplant.

3 small Japanese or Italian eggplants (about 12 ounces)

2 tablespoons canola oil

½ medium yellow onion, finely
chopped (about 1 cup)

1 small tomato, finely chopped
(about ¼ cup)

2 cloves garlic, minced

1 teaspoon cayenne

½ teaspoon coriander seeds,
finely ground

¼ teaspoon cumin seeds, finely
ground

¼ teaspoon ground turmeric

2 small green serrano chiles, cut
lengthwise in half

¾ teaspoon salt

1 pound small or medium shrimp,
peeled and deveined

1 cup canned coconut milk

½ cup water

1½ tablespoons apple cider
vinegar

Slice the eggplants lengthwise in half and then crosswise into 1-inch chunks.

Heat the oil in a large saucepan over medium heat and sauté the onion until softened. Add the tomato, garlic, cayenne, coriander, cumin, and turmeric, and sauté until the tomato has completely disintegrated. If necessary, deglaze the pan by adding a few table-spoons of water and using a spatula to loosen the browned bits if the mixture starts sticking to the bottom.

Add the eggplant, chiles, and salt, and mix well. Cover and cook over low heat until the eggplant is soft, about 10 minutes. Add the shrimp and stir gently. When the shrimp begins to turn pink, add the coconut milk and water. Continue simmering, uncovered, until the shrimp is cooked through, another 5 to 8 minutes. Very gently stir in the vinegar and remove from the heat.

This curry tastes even better the next day. Reheat gently over low heat, stirring carefully once in a while, just until warmed, to prevent overcooking the shrimp.

Serves 4

mussels in a green curry

I created this dish for a magazine photo shoot a few years ago as an interesting alternative to the usual white wine sauce. Buy the freshest mussels possible—choose only those that are tightly closed and smell briny and like the ocean. When you get home, fill a bowl with ice and lay a clean kitchen towel over the ice. If the mussels are in a mesh bag, simply lay the bag over the ice. If they came in a plastic bag, remove the mussels and arrange them over the cold towel. Place this bowl in the refrigerator until you are ready to cook the mussels.

1 pound mussels

¼ teaspoon cumin seeds, freshly ground

½ small tomato

½ cup cilantro leaves

¼ cup mint leaves

1-inch piece fresh ginger

2 small green serrano chiles

2 tablespoons canola oil

½ medium yellow onion, finely chopped (about 1 cup)

1 cup canned coconut milk

Salt

Scrub the mussels well. Pull off any beards and discard any mussels that are not tightly closed.

Using a blender or food processor, grind the cumin, tomato, cilantro, mint, ginger, and chiles to a fine, smooth paste. You may add a few tablespoons of water if needed.

Heat the oil in a medium wok or cast-iron skillet over medium heat, and sauté the onion until golden. Add the green curry paste and sauté until the curry smells cooked and fragrant, 4 to 5 minutes. Add the coconut milk and salt to taste, and bring to a boil. Add the mussels and reduce the heat to low. Toss well, cover, and cook until all the mussels open, about 5 minutes. Discard any that have not opened.

Serve hot with rice or French bread.

Serves **4** as a starter or **2** as a main dish

spicy seared shrimp

This tangy recipe is one of the easiest ways to make shrimp. In fact, I demonstrated the entire recipe—from start to finish—during a five-minute appearance on TV as a guest chef. It takes an extra three minutes to get the marinade ready, so if you can spare eight minutes, you can make a fantastic shrimp dish. Serve either as an appetizer or as a main course with French bread to soak up all the delicious juices. This dish is so colorful on its own, it doesn't even need a garnish.

12 jumbo or 8 ounces large tiger shrimp

½ lemon, juiced

2 cloves garlic, minced

3 tablespoons canola oil, divided

1 tablespoon finely chopped cilantro leaves

½ teaspoon cayenne

½ teaspoon ground turmeric

Salt

Clean and shell the shrimp, leaving the tails on. Rinse. In a shallow bowl, combine the lemon juice, garlic, 1 tablespoon of the oil, the cilantro, cayenne, turmeric, and salt. (Some frozen shrimp are salted, so remember to take that into account.) Stir well and taste—the marinade should be tangy and spicy. Add the shrimp and toss to coat evenly with the marinade.

Heat a large skillet on high heat and add the remaining 2 tablespoons oil. When the oil is smoking, add the shrimp and marinade to the pan. Leave the heat on high. Toss the shrimp several times. Cover the pan while the shrimp cook so all the marinade doesn't evaporate. When the shrimp are just pink, about 5 minutes, remove and arrange them on a platter, pouring any remaining juices over. Do not overcook.

Serve hot or at room temperature.

Serves **4** as an appetizer or **2** as a main dish

NOTE: *You can also barbecue the shrimp. Use wooden skewers that have been soaked in water for half an hour. Skewer the shrimp, draining and reserving the marinade, and barbecue them over high heat until just cooked. Baste with the marinade occasionally.*

shrimp cakes
with ginger and cilantro

These spicy shrimp cakes are a treat for shellfish lovers. It takes a little time to form and fry them, but it's well worth the effort. You can save a little time by buying peeled and deveined frozen shrimp. Prepare ahead by forming the breaded shrimp cakes and refrigerating them overnight, then frying them the next day. Refrigeration will help bind the shrimp mixture together. Just remember to bring them to room temperature before you begin frying.

2 to 3 cups canola oil, divided

½ large yellow onion, minced (about 1 cup)

3 small green serrano chiles, minced

1-inch piece fresh ginger, minced

¼ cup loosely packed cilantro leaves, minced

½ teaspoon cayenne

½ teaspoon ground turmeric

1 small russet potato, boiled until tender (about 4 ounces)

8 ounces medium shrimp, peeled (fresh or frozen)

1 egg, whisked

Salt

½ cup fine dry bread crumbs (make your own with lightly toasted white bread)

Heat 1 teaspoon of oil in a small skillet over medium heat, and lightly sauté the onion, chiles, and ginger until the onion turns golden. It will seem as if there isn't enough oil to really sauté properly, but if you add too much oil now, it will be hard to form the cakes later. Add the cilantro, cayenne, and turmeric, and sauté for 1 more minute. Cool slightly.

Cool, peel, and mash the potato.

Using a food processor, pulse-grind the shrimp until it is lumpy. You may also use a large kitchen knife to roughly chop the shrimp. Combine it with the potato, onion mixture, egg, and salt and mix well. Sometimes the shrimp you buy is already salted, so add as much salt as you think is appropriate and test the mixture before you form all the cakes.

Heat 1 teaspoon of oil in a small skillet, form a tiny shrimp cake, and cook it in the hot oil. Taste this cake and check for salt. Make any adjustments before you proceed with the rest of the recipe.

Wet your palms and form the shrimp cakes. First divide the mixture into 12 balls, then flatten the balls into discs. They will be roughly 1½ inches in diameter and ½ inch thick. Pat the cakes in the bread crumbs, coating well on all sides. The cakes will be loose in texture; this is desirable, as they will be moist and tender when they are fried, not rubbery little hockey pucks!

(continued)

shrimp cakes with
ginger and cilantro
(continued)

In a medium skillet, heat enough oil to come halfway up the sides of the cakes. When the oil begins to smoke, gently place in enough cakes to make one layer. Do not crowd the pan. When they are golden brown on 1 side, after about 3 or 4 minutes, turn them over and brown on the other side. Work in batches until all the cakes are done. Remove the cakes to a plate lined with paper towels.

Serve immediately.

Serves **6**

NOTE: *If you are planning to refrigerate the cakes in order to fry them at a later time, layer them on wax paper so they don't stick to each other, and cover tightly with plastic wrap.*

indian fried fish

When you buy a whole fish in India, it's common practice to reserve the best portions for pan-frying in shallow oil; the rest is used in a curry. This simple, delicious preparation appears on tables at lunchtime in communities all along the coast. The fish may vary, depending on whatever was freshest at the market that day, but the technique is the same. This dish goes particularly well with Mild Fish Stew with Potatoes (page 81) and steamed rice. In India, fried fish is often served alongside a curried fish dish, providing a nice contrast of textures and flavors.

1 pound firm white fish fillets, like catfish or cod, ½ inch thick

2 teaspoons all-purpose flour

1 teaspoon salt

½ teaspoon cayenne

½ teaspoon ground turmeric

2½ to 3 teaspoons lemon juice, depending on the tartness of the lemon

1 teaspoon water

¼ cup canola oil

Lemon wedges for garnish

Rinse and pat dry the fish fillets. In a small bowl, mix together the flour, salt, cayenne, and turmeric. When well combined, add the lemon juice and water to make a thick paste. Taste—it should be spicy, slightly tart, and perfectly salted. Rub the fillets with this mixture, thinly coating all sides well. Set aside for at least 10 minutes and up to 1 hour.

Heat a heavy-bottomed skillet (I like to use my trusty cast-iron pan) over high heat. The skillet can be large enough to hold all the fillets at once, or you can fry the fish in batches. Add the oil and let it heat up well; watch for ripples in the surface signaling that the oil is ready. Keep a spatter screen handy. Gently place the fillets in the oil, turn the heat down to medium, and cover with a screen if the oil is spattering too much. (Do not cover with a solid lid though.)

When the fish is browned and done on one side, about 4 minutes, turn it over and fry on the other side until browned, another 3 to 4 minutes. Remove to plates and serve immediately with a squeeze of lemon.

Serves 4

mild fish stew with potatoes

DISH
33

Fish and potatoes complement each other very well in this comforting Indian stew. I particularly love the way the potatoes soak up the curry. This is one of the few coconut milk curries that doesn't reheat well, mainly because you end up overcooking the fish. The addition of vinegar at the very end of cooking helps to round off and balance all the flavors in the curry. Serve with Goan Savory Crêpes (page 113) as pictured here, or over steamed white rice with Indian Fried Fish (page 79) on the side.

1¼ pounds catfish or cod fillets, at least 1 inch thick

2 medium russet potatoes (about 12 ounces)

2 tablespoons canola oil

½ medium yellow onion, cut into ¼-inch dice (scant 1 cup)

¼ teaspoon ground turmeric

2 small green serrano chiles, cut lengthwise in quarters

3 large cloves garlic, thinly sliced

1 teaspoon finely chopped fresh ginger (about 2-inch piece)

1 cup water

¾ teaspoon salt, divided

One 15-ounce can coconut milk

1 teaspoon apple cider vinegar or rice vinegar

Cut the fish into 2-inch pieces. Peel and then quarter the potatoes lengthwise, then cut them crosswise into 2-inch pieces.

Heat the oil in a large pan over medium heat, and sauté the onion until golden. Add the turmeric and stir. Then add the potatoes, chiles, garlic, and ginger, and stir until the potatoes are well coated with the oil, 2 to 3 minutes. Add the water and ½ teaspoon of the salt, and bring to a boil. Reduce heat to a simmer, cover, and cook till the potatoes are tender, about 10 minutes.

Add the coconut milk, fish pieces, and the remaining ¼ teaspoon salt and bring the stew back to a simmer. Cook until the fish is opaque and slightly springy to the touch, about 5 minutes. Stir in the vinegar, let sit for 5 minutes, and serve.

Serves 4

DISH
34

baked fish in a spice broth

This is a simple yet elegant dish, perfect for weeknight entertaining. It's based on an Indian technique in which you place all the ingredients in a pot, cover tightly, and cook over low heat, usually a wood fire. I prefer to start the dish with a flavorful spice broth, then bake it in the oven. All that's left to do is toss a green salad, warm the bread, and chill a bottle of white wine.

1½ pounds lingcod or halibut fillets, at least 1 inch thick

½ teaspoon coriander seeds

3 tablespoons canola oil

3 large shallots, finely minced (about ½ cup)

¼ teaspoon finely grated fresh ginger (about ½-inch piece)

¼ teaspoon finely grated garlic (about 1 clove)

¼ to ½ teaspoon cayenne

1 cup water

½ teaspoon salt

1 medium Roma tomato, finely chopped (about ½ cup)

1 tablespoon minced cilantro leaves

Lemon wedges for garnish

Preheat the oven to 350°F.

Cut the fish into 3-inch square pieces. In a small skillet, toast the coriander seeds over low heat until browned and fragrant. Cool and finely grind the seeds.

Heat the oil in a large pan over medium heat, add the shallots, and stir until they turn golden. Add the ginger, garlic, and cayenne to taste, and stir constantly over medium heat for another 30 seconds, taking care that the mixture doesn't burn. Add the water, salt, and ground coriander, and bring to a boil.

Place the fish pieces in a casserole large enough to hold them in a single layer, and sprinkle the tomatoes evenly over the top. Pour the spicy broth on top and bake until the fish is cooked through but not overdone, about 10 minutes. You can use a fork to test one of the pieces of fish discreetly; if it flakes easily, it is time to remove the dish from the oven.

Serve sprinkled with the cilantro and garnished with the lemon wedges.

Serves 4

chapter **6:** salads and raitas

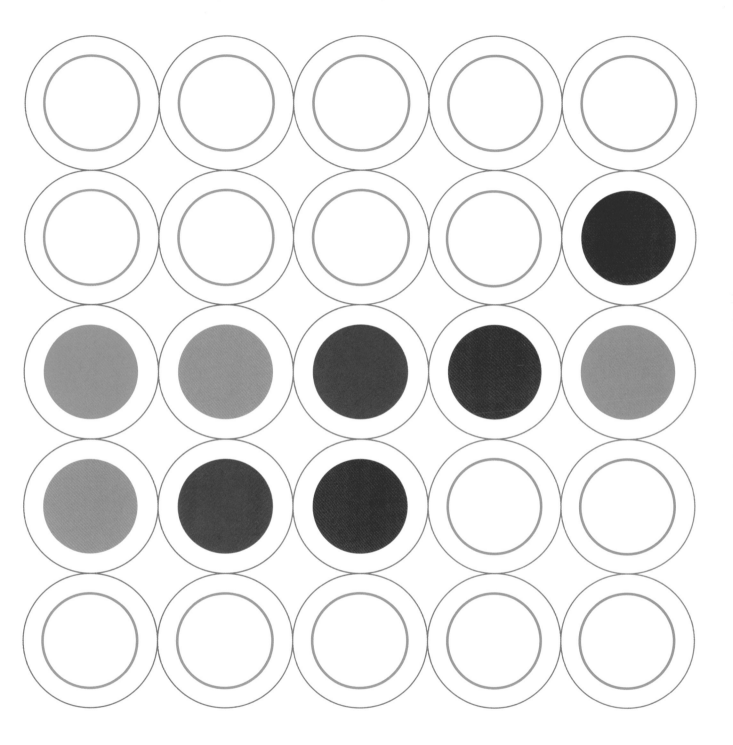

dishes **35—43**

The concept of salad as a stand-alone dish doesn't really exist in traditional Indian cuisine. A "salad" in India is a tangy, sometimes spicy relish, eaten in small quantities to complement the rest of the meal, following the principles of Ayurveda. According to this ancient science, a balanced meal should contain six tastes—sweet, sour, salty, bitter, astringent, and pungent—and a variety of textures and food groups. Salads and raitas help fill those requirements.

A raita is an Indian salad with a yogurt dressing, adding all the nutritional benefits of that superfood. And contrary to popular belief, the role of a raita is not to cool down a spicy Indian meal; a raita can itself be quite spicy.

These recipes yield about four small portions, to be served with a meal. But they're so good, I wouldn't be surprised if you'd want to eat a bowlful for lunch.

black-eyed pea salad with ginger and red onion

This is one of those rare Indian salads that makes a meal in itself. I usually bring a large bowl as my contribution to summer potlucks. If you use canned peas, you can put this salad together in literally a few minutes.

1½ cups dried black-eyed peas or two 15-ounce cans black-eyed peas, drained

1 cup finely chopped ripe tomatoes (about 2 medium tomatoes)

½ cup finely chopped red onion (about 1 small onion)

¼ cup finely chopped cilantro leaves

2 tablespoons lime juice, or more to taste

1 teaspoon finely chopped fresh ginger (about 2-inch piece)

1 small green serrano chile, minced (seed it first if you prefer)

1 teaspoon cumin seeds, finely ground

½ teaspoon cayenne

Salt

1 tablespoon canola oil

¼ teaspoon mustard seeds

If using dried black-eyed peas, soak them for 6 to 8 hours or overnight, with water to cover.

Bring a large pot of salted water to a boil. Drain the soaked peas and add them to the pot. Cook until they are tender but not falling apart, about 30 minutes. Drain and remove to a medium bowl. Cool.

If using canned peas, skip the above steps and proceed with the rest of the recipe.

Add the tomatoes, onion, cilantro, lime juice, ginger, chile, cumin, cayenne, and salt to taste (remember canned peas already have salt in them) to the cooked, cooled peas and toss well. You can increase the amount of lime juice in the recipe if you like.

Make the tadka: Heat the oil in a small skillet or butter warmer over high heat. When the oil begins to smoke, add the mustard seeds, covering the pan with a lid or spatter screen. After the seeds have finished popping, pour the tadka over the peas and toss well.

Serve cold or at room temperature.

Serves 4 to 6

crunchy cucumber salad with crushed peanuts

My mother showed me this salad recipe twenty years ago, and I still make it exactly the same way. Fresh and complex tasting at the same time, it's hard to improve upon. Anyone who eats this salad at my home ends up asking for the recipe, so I'd thought I'd share it with you as well.

2 English or other unwaxed cucumbers, chopped into ¼-inch dice (about 3 cups)

1 medium green serrano chile, minced (seed first if you prefer)

½ cup peanuts, preferably raw, but toasted, unsalted ones will do

2 tablespoons lemon juice, or more if needed

1 teaspoon salt

½ to ¾ teaspoon sugar

⅛ teaspoon cayenne

1 tablespoon canola oil

¼ teaspoon mustard seeds

Place the diced cucumbers in a medium bowl along with the chile. Using a coffee grinder or food processor, pulse the peanuts until they are reduced to a coarse powder. (You don't want big chunks of peanuts, nor do you want a fine powder; stop grinding somewhere in between!) Add the peanuts to the cucumbers along with the lemon juice, salt, and sugar, and mix well. Taste and adjust the salt, sugar, and lemon juice as needed. The salad should be slightly tart.

Make the tadka: Place the cayenne in a little pile on top of the salad. Do not stir it in yet. Heat the oil in a small skillet or butter warmer over high heat. When it begins to smoke, add the mustard seeds, covering the pan with a lid or spatter screen. As soon as the seeds stop sputtering, pour the oil over the cayenne. Stir the dressing in and serve at room temperature or cold.

Serves 4

tangy shredded cabbage salad

Fresh, crunchy, tangy, and spicy, this salad is an excellent way to get your weekly serving of a vegetable known for its cancer-fighting properties. Think of this salad as an Indian-style slaw; it will make a nice addition to your barbecue repertoire.

2 cups tightly packed, shredded green cabbage (use the large holes of the grater)

1 small green serrano chile, minced

2 tablespoons lemon juice, or more as needed

1 teaspoon salt

½ teaspoon sugar

1 tablespoon canola oil

½ teaspoon mustard seeds

In a medium bowl, toss together the cabbage, chile, lemon juice, salt, and sugar. Taste and adjust the seasoning. You are looking for a well-balanced, sweet-and-sour taste.

Make the tadka: Heat the oil in a small skillet or butter warmer over high heat. When the oil begins to smoke, add the mustard seeds, covering the pan with a lid or spatter screen. When the seeds stop popping, immediately pour the oil over the cabbage salad and toss well. Let the salad sit for at least 15 minutes before serving, to allow the flavors to blossom.

Serve cold or at room temperature.

Serves **2** to **4**

crispy okra raita

Oddly enough, children in India love okra. But it's hardly surprising; whether sautéed, fried, or stuffed, the vegetable is prepared in a way that makes its texture pleasing rather than gooey. In this recipe, for instance, the okra becomes crunchy and addictive on its own; stirred into spiced yogurt, it's even better. I hope it makes an okra lover out of you, too. I could eat this all on its own, but it is also a wonderful addition to any Indian meal and goes especially well with Thalipeeth (page 107) as pictured here.

8 ounces fresh or frozen, cut okra

6 tablespoons canola oil, divided

1 cup plain whole or low-fat yogurt

¾ to 1 teaspoon salt

½ teaspoon sugar

⅛ teaspoon cayenne

⅛ teaspoon ground turmeric

½ teaspoon mustard seeds

Wash the okra and towel dry each one thoroughly. Slice into ¼-inch-thick rounds. If using frozen, do not thaw.

Heat 5 tablespoons of the oil in a large skillet over medium heat. When the oil is very hot, add the okra, toss, and let sizzle. Toss occasionally. The okra will slowly turn crisp and brown. (The frozen okra may not get crisp; this is okay, but make sure to brown it well.) Once all the okra is well browned, remove to a paper towel–lined platter and set aside until ready to serve.

Make the tadka: Whisk the yogurt with the salt (to taste) and sugar. Place the cayenne and turmeric in a small pile on the raita, but do not mix in yet. Heat the remaining 1 tablespoon oil in a butter warmer or small skillet over high heat. When the oil begins to smoke, add the mustard seeds, covering the pan with a lid or spatter screen. After the mustard seeds stop sputtering, pour the hot oil directly on top of the cayenne and turmeric powder. (This cooks the powdered spices without burning them.) Do not stir the dressing in yet.

For presentation just prior to serving, place the crisp okra on top of the dressing. Stir the okra and dressing into the yogurt while serving.

Serves **2** to **4**

fire-roasted eggplant raita

Bharta *is a generic Indian term for roasted eggplant preparations. While the eggplant is always cooked over an open flame and then skinned, the final presentation varies with the region. It may be sautéed with tomatoes, mixed with fresh peas, or stirred into fresh yogurt, as it is in this recipe from the state of Maharashtra. I think this is by far the most flavorful way to make a bharta. The yogurt forms a perfect backdrop for the wonderfully smoky notes provided by the roasted eggplant. Serve with Chapati (page 109) and Punjabi Red Beans (page 43). This raita also makes a terrific dip for crackers or pita bread.*

1 medium Italian eggplant (about 1 pound)

3 tablespoons canola oil, divided

½ cup plain whole or low-fat yogurt

½ teaspoon salt

¼ teaspoon sugar

2 tablespoons minced red onion

2 tablespoons finely chopped cilantro leaves

1 medium green serrano chile, finely chopped (optional)

¼ teaspoon cayenne

½ teaspoon mustard seeds

Smoke the eggplant under the broiler, over an open stovetop flame, or on an outdoor grill. First, wash the eggplant and dry it thoroughly. Using the tip of a small knife, pierce the skin in a couple of places and rub it lightly with 1 tablespoon of the oil. Place the eggplant over the flame or under the broiler. Turn frequently so it blackens evenly on all sides. In 15 to 20 minutes, it will turn soft and will collapse on itself when touched. Remove to a bowl and set aside to cool.

In a medium bowl, lightly beat the yogurt with the salt and sugar. Then stir in the onion and cilantro and the chile (if using).

Skin the eggplant when completely cool. The skin should peel off easily, leaving the wonderful smoky flesh behind. Save the juices that have collected in the bowl. Add the juices and the skinned eggplant to the yogurt mixture and combine well. Don't mash the eggplant too much; the naturally lumpy texture is desirable.

Make the tadka: Place the cayenne in a small pile on the raita, but do not mix in yet. Heat the remaining 2 tablespoons of the oil in a small skillet or butter warmer over high heat. When the oil begins to smoke, add the mustard seeds, covering the pan with a lid or spatter screen. After the seeds stop sputtering, pour the hot oil directly on top of the cayenne. Swirl the dressing decoratively into the yogurt just before serving. Serve cold or at room temperature.

Serves 4

spinach raita
with toasted cumin

It's easy to eat a whole bowl of this raita all on its own. Besides, it's a delicious way to get your serving of greens! I favor fresh spinach, but you may substitute frozen if you like. Try it as a dip for crudités at your next picnic or alongside Black-Eyed Peas in a Spicy Goan Curry (page 40).

4 ounces baby spinach or
   5 ounces frozen spinach

½ teaspoon cumin seeds

1 cup plain whole or low-fat
   yogurt

2 tablespoons minced red onion

¾ to 1 teaspoon salt

¼ teaspoon finely grated fresh
   ginger (about ½-inch piece)

Rinse the baby spinach and place it in a saucepan with the water still clinging to the leaves. Cover and steam the leaves until tender but still bright green. Place in a strainer to cool and drain. If using frozen spinach, place in a saucepan with ¼ cup water and cook over low heat for 5 minutes. Drain.

Toast the cumin seeds in a small skillet over low heat until they turn dark and fragrant. Cool and grind them.

In a small bowl, stir the yogurt together with the onion, salt, ginger, and the ground cumin.

Squeeze the cooled spinach to remove excess water and finely chop it. Add this to the yogurt mixture and stir thoroughly. Chill until ready to serve.

Serves **4**

DISH
41

butternut squash raita with ground mustard

This unusual raita combines cool yogurt with freshly ground mustard seeds to add a mild heat reminiscent of horseradish. It's a treat for the eye as well, thanks to all the different colors, including the beautiful golden squash. Be careful while prepping the squash—I prefer to cut it in half first and then peel each half separately, because trying to cut a whole, slippery peeled squash seems to me like a downright dangerous operation!

1 small butternut squash (about 1 pound)

½ cup water

½ teaspoon mustard seeds

1 cup plain whole or low-fat yogurt, whisked

2 tablespoons minced cilantro leaves

¾ teaspoon salt

¼ teaspoon sugar

1 tablespoon canola oil

½ teaspoon cumin seeds

1 small green serrano chile, finely chopped (optional)

Peel and cut the squash into 1-inch cubes. Place the cubes in a medium saucepan with the water, cover, and steam over medium heat until soft, about 10 minutes. Cool slightly.

Mash the squash lightly with a fork. (Do not mash completely—a lumpy texture is desirable.) Place the mustard seeds on a clean, dry cutting board. Using the back of a skillet, crush the seeds. Stir the ground mustard seeds, yogurt, cilantro, salt, and sugar into the mashed squash.

Make the tadka: Heat the oil in a small skillet or butter warmer over high heat. When the oil begins to smoke, add the cumin seeds, covering the pan with a lid or spatter screen. After the seeds stop sputtering, lower the heat and add the chile, if using. When the chile is toasted, pour the dressing over the raita. Stir and serve.

Serves **4** to **6**

shredded carrot raita
with raisins and walnuts

Even if you're not a big fan of raw carrots, this sweet raita will have you going back for seconds. Be sure to pick sweet, tender carrots for this recipe. Serve with Roasted Lamb with Burnt Onions (page 57).

2 tablespoons raisins

6 walnut halves

1½ cups plain whole or low-fat yogurt

1 tablespoon minced mint leaves, divided

1 teaspoon salt

¼ to ½ teaspoon cayenne

½ teaspoon sugar

2 cups grated carrots (about 2 medium)

Soak the raisins in warm water to cover for at least 30 minutes and up to overnight. Chop the walnuts coarsely.

In a medium bowl, whisk together the yogurt, half of the mint, the salt, cayenne, and sugar. Taste and add more sugar if the yogurt is too tart. Add a few tablespoons of water if the raita seems too thick.

Drain the raisins and add them along with the carrots and walnuts to the yogurt dressing. Stir well and garnish with the remaining mint.

Serve cold.

Serves **4** to **6**

roasted onion raita

DISH
43

I remember visiting my grandmother's village as a child; the aromas from her kitchen still linger with me. One of them was the smoky fragrance of onions roasting. My aunt would toss a whole onion into the hot embers of the wood-burning stove. By the time the rest of the dinner was done, the onion would have slowly roasted to perfection, ready to be stirred into thick, homemade yogurt. In fact, you may want to try that trick at your next barbecue. This simple raita is perfect as a dip for samosas or pakoras or to accompany Lamb Chops with a Spicy Rub (page 54).

1 medium red onion, unpeeled

⅛ teaspoon cumin seeds

½ cup plain whole or low-fat yogurt

½ teaspoon salt

¼ teaspoon sugar

Roast the onion over an open flame or under a broiler, turning often, until it is well blistered all over and soft inside, about 10 minutes. Set aside until cool enough to handle. Peel and mince the onion, retaining all the juices.

Toast the cumin seeds in a dry skillet until brown and fragrant. Remove to a cutting board and coarsely crush them using the back of a spoon.

Whisk together the cumin, yogurt, salt, and sugar. Add the onion along with its juices, stir, and taste. Adjust the salt and sugar as needed.

Serve at room temperature or cold.

Serves 4

chapter **7:** rice and bread

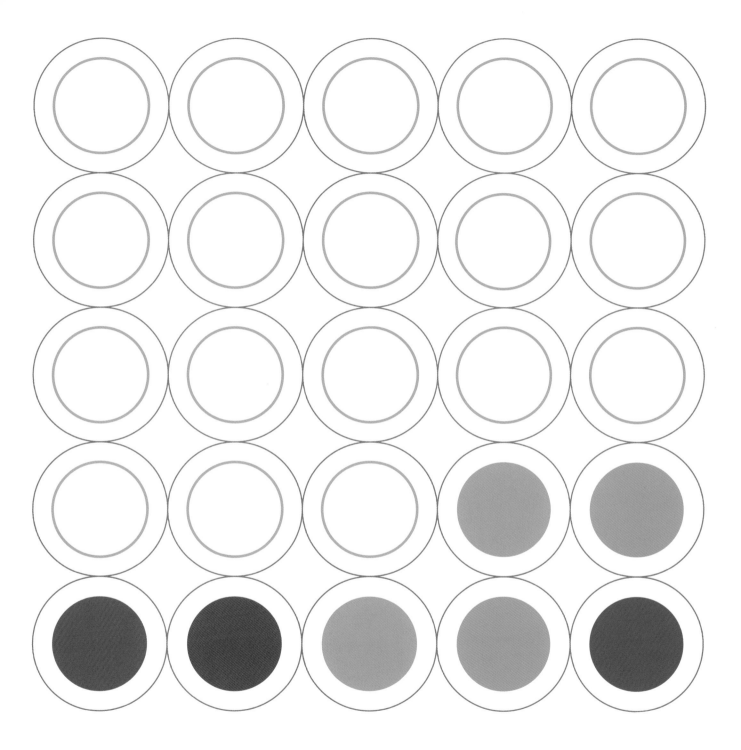

dishes 44—50

Rice in India comes in all shapes and sizes, from the tiny *kalijeera* grown in the east to the fat red grains of Goa, which my family lovingly refers to as "bullet rice." For the recipes in this section, use a long-grain white rice like basmati. And since steamed white rice goes with just about anything in this book, here's my simple method for cooking it:

Rinse the white basmati rice a couple of times to clean the grains and get rid of some of the starch. To every cup of rice, add 1¾ cups of water. Bring to a boil, cover, and reduce heat to a simmer. Cook for 15 minutes, turn off the heat, and let sit, covered, for an additional 5 minutes. Don't uncover the pot during the cooking or resting period. Fluff with a fork, and it's ready to serve. Note that the cooking time will stay the same for up to 5 cups of rice.

Most people are familiar with Indian flatbreads like naan, but I wanted to turn the spotlight on some breads that are relatively unknown yet truly deserving of attention. The exception here, of course, is the chapati, which, like steamed white rice, is a staple that goes with just about any Indian menu.

marathi yellow fried rice

Like most fried-rice recipes, this is usually made with leftover rice. In fact, my mother would often convert the previous night's steamed rice into this comforting dish for breakfast. Delicious on its own, you can also serve it with Crispy Okra Raita (page 93) for an easy supper. This rice tastes great even at room temperature, so it makes excellent picnic food.

¼ cup canola oil

½ teaspoon mustard seeds

2 medium green serrano chiles, sliced in ⅛-inch-thick rounds

1 medium red onion, cut into ½-inch dice (about 1½ cups)

½ teaspoon ground turmeric

5 cups cooked white rice, cooled

1 tablespoon lemon juice

1½ to 2½ teaspoons salt

½ teaspoon sugar

¼ cup tightly packed cilantro leaves, minced

Make the tadka: Heat the oil in a large wok over high heat. When the oil begins to smoke, add the mustard seeds, covering the pan with a lid or spatter screen. After the seeds have stopped sputtering, add the chiles. When the chiles are toasted, add the onion and stir-fry until the onion is golden around the edges. Add the turmeric, stir well, and take off the heat.

Add the rice, lemon juice, salt, and sugar to the pan, and toss until all the ingredients are mixed thoroughly and all the rice grains are yellow. If you usually salt your rice while steaming it, you will need the lesser of the 2 amounts of salt while making this fried rice.

Return the wok to low heat, cover, and steam until the flavors have blended, about 5 minutes. Garnish with the cilantro and serve, or cool to room temperature, cover, and take to a picnic.

Serves **4**

lentil-rice pilaf

DISH
45

When I was in college, I had a friend whose family employed an extraordinary cook by the name of Bashir. Being a Muslim, Bashir cooked with techniques and ingredients that were unfamiliar and fascinating to me. Needless to say, I didn't decline a single invitation to lunch at my friend's house. Bashir often served a pilaf similar to this one with his meat curries; you can serve it with Indian Brown Beef Stew (page 47) or Chicken in Cashew Nut Sauce (page 65).

1½ cups long-grain white rice, preferably basmati

½ cup small brown lentils, picked over

2 tablespoons canola oil

½ teaspoon cumin seeds

1 small yellow onion, halved and thinly sliced (about 1½ cups)

2 small green serrano chiles, sliced in ⅛-inch-thick rounds

1 tablespoon unsalted butter

4 cups hot water or chicken broth

1 medium tomato, chopped (about ½ cup)

1½ teaspoons salt

Rinse and soak the rice and lentils together in cold water for at least 10 minutes while you prepare the rest of the ingredients. Drain well.

Make the tadka: Heat the oil in a large stockpot over high heat. When it begins to smoke, add the cumin seeds, covering the pan with a lid or spatter screen. After the seeds are done sputtering, add the onion, chiles, and butter, and sauté over medium heat until the onion turns golden brown.

Add the drained rice and lentils, and stir gently until all the rice is coated with the oil and butter, 2 to 3 minutes. Add the water, tomato, and salt and stir well. Bring to a boil, cover, and turn the heat down to a simmer. Cook, covered, for 15 minutes. Remove from the heat and let the pilaf sit, covered, for another 5 minutes. Do not open the lid during the cooking period or resting time, as the rice is absorbing any remaining moisture in the pot. Fluff with a fork and serve hot.

Serves 6

turkey and basmati rice pilaf

This hearty pilaf is traditionally made with ground goat meat in India. My version is lighter, yet just as tasty, and I often make it as a one-pot TV dinner in our home. I ladle out piping hot bowlfuls and we all curl up to watch The Lion King *for the 127th time with our toddler, who, by the way, also loves this pilaf.*

1½ cups long-grain white rice, preferably basmati

2 tablespoons canola oil

1½ teaspoons cumin seeds, divided

1 small red onion, thinly sliced (about 1 cup)

1 tablespoon unsalted butter

1 teaspoon coriander seeds

1 teaspoon finely grated fresh ginger (about 2-inch piece)

1 teaspoon finely grated garlic (about 2 large cloves)

1 pound ground turkey

1 medium carrot, cut into ¼-inch pieces

½ cup frozen peas

½ teaspoon ground turmeric

2 teaspoons salt

3½ cups hot water

Minced mint leaves for garnish

Rinse the rice and set aside to drain in a strainer.

Make the tadka: Heat the oil in a large stockpot over high heat. When the oil begins to smoke, add ½ teaspoon of the cumin seeds, covering the pan with a lid or spatter screen. After the seeds are done sputtering, add the onion and butter and sauté over medium heat until the onion turns golden.

While the onion is cooking, heat a small skillet and roast the remaining 1 teaspoon cumin seeds over low heat until dark and fragrant. Remove the seeds from the pan and set aside to cool. Now add the coriander and slowly roast over low heat until dark brown. Make sure you don't try to hurry the process and end up with burnt spices instead of aromatically roasted ones! When the coriander seeds have cooled, grind them with the cumin seeds and set aside.

Add the ginger and garlic to the golden onions and sauté over low heat until the mixture smells fragrant, 3 to 4 minutes. Add the turkey, carrot, peas, and turmeric. Turn the heat up to high and brown the turkey, stirring constantly and breaking up any lumps. Add the ground roasted cumin and coriander, and continue stirring over high heat until all the liquid has evaporated.

Add the drained rice and salt, and stir gently until well mixed. Add the water, stir, and bring to a boil. Cover the pot and turn the heat down to a simmer. Cook, covered, for 15 minutes. Remove from the heat and let the pilaf sit, covered, for another 5 minutes. Do not open the lid during the cooking period or resting time, as the rice is absorbing any remaining moisture in the pot. Fluff with a fork and serve hot, garnished with minced mint.

Serves **6**

thalipeeth

This vegetable-studded bread requires no kneading or rising; just mix the ingredients and spread the dough on a skillet. In fact, the word "thalipeeth" loosely translates as "skillet bread." My father would often make us a batch when no one had the energy to cook a full meal, leading to his title as the "Undisputed Thalipeeth King." This nutritious flatbread keeps very well for two to three days. That's why one of my students usually brings some along on camping trips, referring to it as "veggie jerky." You may double or triple the recipe as needed.

1 medium English cucumber

1½ cups whole wheat flour

½ teaspoon cumin seeds

1½ teaspoons salt

½ to 1 teaspoon cayenne

1 teaspoon sesame seeds

½ teaspoon ground turmeric

9 tablespoons canola or peanut oil, divided

1 large green serrano chile, finely chopped

Peel the cucumber, and then grate it using the large holes on the grater. You want about 1 cup.

Place the flour in a large bowl. Crush the cumin seeds slightly by rubbing between the palms of your hands to release their aromatic oils, and then add to the flour. Stir in the salt, cayenne, sesame seeds, and turmeric, and mix until well blended. Add 3 tablespoons of the oil, the cucumber, and chile, and mix in well. Add a few tablespoons of water, if necessary, to make a sticky dough. You don't have to knead this dough at all; merely bring all the ingredients together. Halve the dough and form into 2 balls.

Place 1 tablespoon of oil in the center of a cold, heavy, medium skillet. I prefer to use cast iron, but you may also use a nonstick one. Coat your palms with oil as well. Place 1 of the dough balls in the center of the oil on the skillet and, using both your hands, gently press it out into a large, even circle about 5 inches in diameter. Make sure it is of even thickness all around, about ½ inch thick. Using your forefinger or the handle of a wooden spoon, make 4 evenly spaced 1-inch holes in the thalipeeth. Fill these little "wells" with oil. Cover the skillet and place over medium-low heat. After about 5 minutes, uncover and check. If the bread is well browned on the bottom, carefully turn it over. This time, leave the bread uncovered. The bread is done when it is browned well on both sides, about 10 minutes more. When making the second thalipeeth, remember that the skillet will be hot—you can either wait till it cools down, or proceed very carefully. Oil the pan again and repeat the above steps.

Makes **2**

chapati

This is the daily bread of Indians, from peasants to princes. A hot chapati right off the skillet is the sensual equivalent of a warm, freshly baked loaf of bread. Indians eat this simple flatbread with practically anything—dals and curries, fried eggs, even sweets like Shrikhand with Yogurt Cheese, Saffron, and Pistachios (page 119). Making chapatis does take a little time, but to keep it manageable, my recipe makes only ten. Don't be disappointed if your first attempts are far from perfect. When I first learned to make chapatis, I was rolling them out in the shape of Australia, as my brother loved to point out.

1½ cups whole wheat flour

½ cup all-purpose flour, plus extra for dusting

1 teaspoon salt

1 cup warm water

5 teaspoons unsalted butter, melted (optional)

You can either use a stand mixer or knead this dough by hand. Stir the two flours and salt together in a medium bowl until well mixed. Gradually add the water, using more or less as needed, mixing all the time (on low speed if using the mixer), until the dough comes together in a ball. Knead well in the mixer or on a flour-dusted work surface until the dough is smooth, elastic, and very pliant, about 10 minutes by hand, less if using a mixer. Set aside to rest, covered with a clean cloth or plastic wrap, for 10 minutes or up to 4 hours.

Divide the dough into 10 equal-sized balls. Dust a work surface with flour, and use your fingers to slightly flatten each ball of dough. Keep the balls of dough covered with a clean, dry cloth. Using a rolling pin, roll each one out into a round chapati about 5 inches in diameter. To achieve a perfect circle, rotate the chapati a quarter turn each time you roll. Dust with flour as you go.

Heat a dry, heavy skillet over medium-high heat until very hot (a drop of water should sizzle right off) and place a chapati on it. In about 1 minute, the surface of the chapati will form tiny bubbles; turn it over. After another minute, remove it and roast over an open flame. To do this, turn on a second burner to a medium-high flame. Using a pair of tongs, place the chapati, first side down, directly on the flame. (Don't worry, the chapati will not burn; it cooks within a few seconds.) It should puff up like a balloon. When it is fully puffed, remove it immediately. If you like, smear it with a little butter.

(continued)

If you don't have a gas stove, then finish cooking the chapati on the skillet. You will miss out on the drama of the puffing bread, but the results will be the same. After you turn the chapati over the first time, cook it until it roasts slightly on the second side, 1 minute more. Then, using a balled-up kitchen towel, press down on the edges of the circle. This should cook the edges of the bread and make it puff up slightly. If you spy steam escaping from any puncture on the surface of the chapati, hold the kitchen towel down on that spot— this helps to trap hot air inside the bread, cooking it from inside. Don't keep the bread on the hot skillet for too long, as this will over-cook and dry out the bread, making it more like cracker bread!

Chapatis are best eaten right after they are made, but you can keep them up to 24 hours. Make sure to store the cooled breads in an airtight container or in a resealable plastic bag, separated by pieces of parchment. Reheat in the microwave, wrapped in a paper towel, or on a hot skillet.

Makes **10**

NOTE: *It is best to roll and cook the chapatis one at a time. If you roll them all out prior to roasting them, they will most definitely dry out. If you have access to* aata, *sometimes spelled "atta" (Indian whole wheat flour), please do substitute it here for both of the flours.*

dal poories

DISH
49

In most Indian households, poories are reserved for special occasions. As you deep-fry this unleavened bread, it magically balloons up, evoking oohs and aahs from everyone present. My recipe mixes a spiced dal paste into the dough to make these already delicious morsels even more festive. Serve with any of the raitas (pages 93 to 98) for breakfast, or add poories to a bread basket at your next Indian meal.

¼ cup dried yellow split peas

8 green onions, coarsely chopped (about ½ cup)

1¼ cups all-purpose flour, plus extra for dusting

½ teaspoon cumin seeds

1 teaspoon salt

1 teaspoon cayenne

1 teaspoon sesame seeds

¼ teaspoon ground turmeric

Canola or peanut oil for deep frying

Rinse and soak the split peas in water to cover for 20 minutes. Drain. Using a food processor, grind together the peas and green onions to a smooth paste. You may use a few tablespoons of water if necessary while grinding, but make sure the texture remains paste-like and not that of a purée.

Place the 1¼ cups flour in a large bowl. Crush the cumin seeds slightly by rubbing between the palms of your hands to release their aromatic oils. Add to the flour along with the salt, cayenne, sesame seeds, and turmeric, and stir until well mixed. Mix in the split pea and onion paste. Add a few tablespoons of water only if the mixture is still too dry and not coming together in a ball. Knead until the dough is smooth and soft, but not sticky, 1 to 2 minutes. If it does become sticky, rub your palms with a little oil and knead the dough again. Depending on how loose your split pea paste is, you may actually require more flour instead of water to make the dough smooth. Set aside to rest, covered with plastic wrap, while you heat the oil.

Add enough oil to a deep wok or pan so as to completely submerge a poori—about 3 inches deep. I like using the smallest wok that will comfortably fit a 4-inch poori—that way I don't waste a lot of oil. Heat the oil over medium heat until very hot, almost smoking, about 370°F on a deep-fat thermometer.

Divide the dough into 15 portions and roll each into a ball. Dust the work surface with very little flour and, using your fingers, press down each ball until it is flattened and resembles a small disc.

(continued)

Using a rolling pin, roll out each disc into a 4-inch circle. It is more important to make them of an even thickness rather than trying to get them as thin as possible. Cover the rest of the dough balls with a dry, clean kitchen towel as you work. Don't stack the poories one over the other, but place them, without touching, on a very lightly floured sheet pan and remember to keep them covered with a dry cloth to keep them from drying out.

Fry the poories by slipping one into the hot oil carefully; it will naturally sink to the bottom. As the poori begins to surface, use a slotted spoon to keep flicking hot oil on top of it. The idea is to keep hot oil on the entire poori at all times. It should puff up like a balloon. When fully puffed, turn it over for a few seconds to color it a little on the other side. Use the slotted spoon to lift the poori, drain off all the oil, and remove it to a paper towel–lined platter. Repeat with the other poories. Fry 1 poori at a time unless you have a large wok and are feeling fairly confident about the technique. Serve immediately.

Makes **15**

NOTE: *You can roll and fry simultaneously. Or, if you prefer, you can roll out all the poories first and then begin frying.*

goan savory crêpes

You may not be able to pronounce suloliyos, *but you can certainly make these savory Goan crêpes with little effort. They're perfect for soaking up any of the coconut-milk curries in this book (pages 28 and 73) or serving with honey for breakfast. The traditional recipe is a lengthy process, requiring you to soak rice in water overnight, then grind it to a fine paste with fresh coconut. But I like to eat these crêpes often, so I simplified the recipe to the point where you can whip them out in ten minutes—just make sure your pantry is stocked with coconut milk and rice flour.*

1 cup fine rice flour (see Note)

1 tablespoon sugar

½ teaspoon salt

1 cup canned coconut milk

1 egg, whisked

½ cup water

Canola oil

In a medium bowl, stir the flour, sugar, and salt together. In a separate bowl, whisk the coconut milk and egg together and mix into the flour. Add the water and whisk to make sure there are no lumps in the batter. This is a thinner crêpe batter than you may be used to; it has the consistency of half-and-half.

Heat an 8-inch nonstick skillet over medium-low heat. (You can use a larger skillet, but the edges of an 8-inch skillet help define the round shape and exact thickness of the crêpe.) Dip a paper towel in the oil and wipe the inside of the skillet, or use a pan spray to get a very light film of oil on the pan. Pour ¼ cup of batter in the center of the pan and immediately swirl the pan in a clockwise motion to spread the batter out into a thin, lacy, 8-inch crêpe.

Cover and steam until little bubbles appear on the surface of the crêpe, about 2 minutes. Cook only on 1 side. Remove to a platter and cover with a domed lid to keep warm. Prepare the rest of the crêpes similarly, making sure to wipe the pan with the oiled paper towel between each crêpe. It is okay to stack them; they do not stick together as long as you don't let the lid sweat.

Serve hot or at room temperature. If you are making them ahead of time, store at room temperature for up to 2 hours. Do not reheat.

Makes **12**

NOTE: *Rice flour is simply raw rice ground very finely. If you cannot find any in your grocery store, make your own by grinding a medium-grained rice to a fine powder in a food processor.*

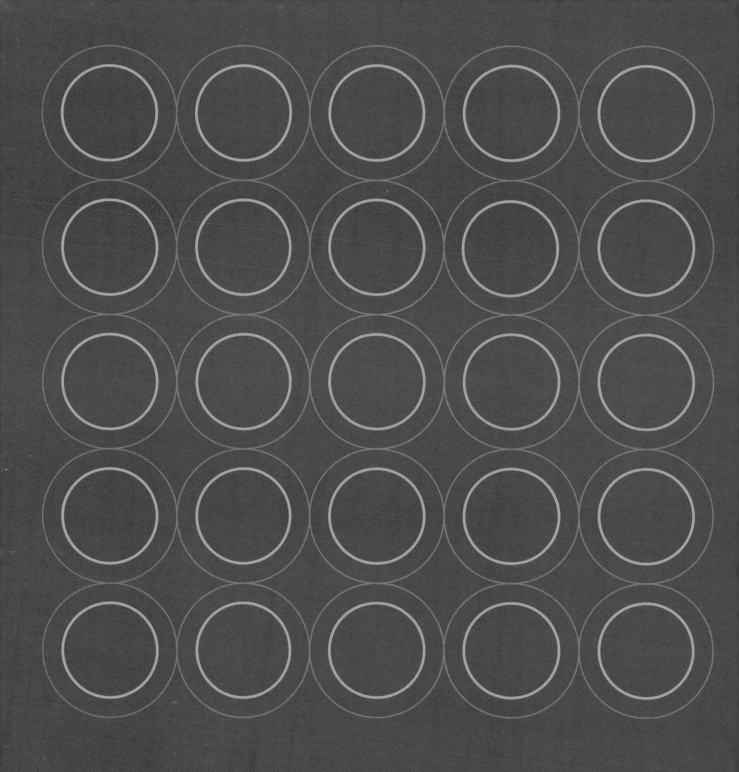

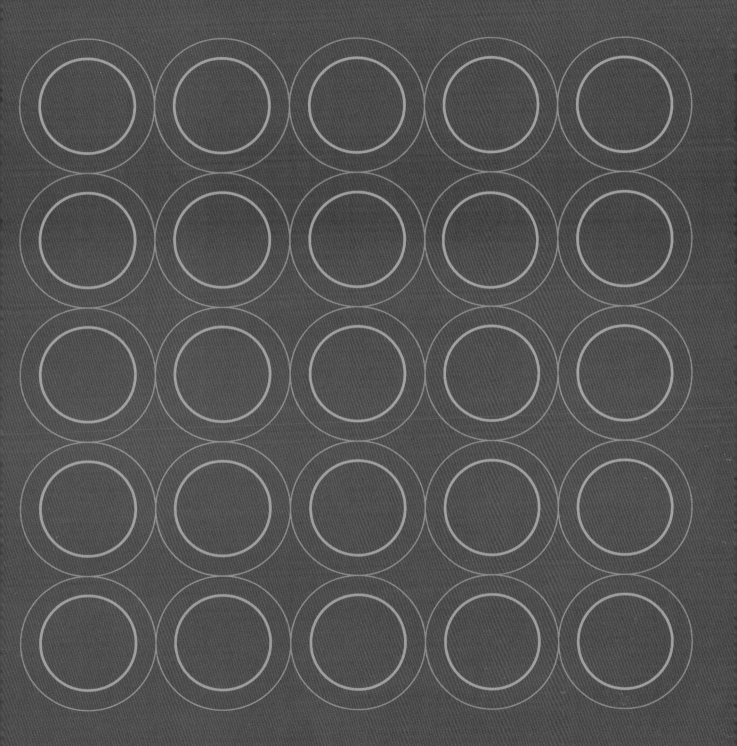

chapter **8**: sweets

Indians love their sweets, but don't necessarily end a meal with them. Sweet dishes are eaten as a snack any time of the day in India. Some communities even serve them as the first course, following the Ayurvedic principle that since sugar is digested first, it should be eaten first. I certainly have no problem with that!

I should mention here that these dessert recipes are a bonus—they don't count toward the main fifty recipes. That's because they require two new spices: saffron and cardamom. Like the other five spices, these should also be readily available at supermarkets and health food stores. Please buy whole cardamom pods as opposed to already peeled cardamom seeds; you will ensure a fresher flavor. Similarly, buy your saffron as "threads," not as a powder—they are much easier to work with. Store both spices in airtight containers in a dark cupboard.

shrikhand with yogurt cheese, saffron, and pistachios

Shrikhand is one of those rare desserts that's not only yummy but virtually guilt free. The only fat here comes from the whole-milk yogurt. You could also use low-fat yogurt, but it yields less yogurt cheese and you will have to adjust the sugar accordingly. So make a batch of this thick, creamy dessert, place it in the refrigerator, and reach in for a helping any time the craving hits.

4 quarts whole-milk yogurt

5 whole green cardamom pods

1 teaspoon saffron threads

1 cup sugar

3 tablespoons coarsely chopped raw pistachios

Line a large strainer with a double thickness of cheesecloth, and place the yogurt in it. Bring the ends of the cloth together and tie into a bundle. Set the strainer over a deep bowl and place in the refrigerator for 8 hours. All the whey will drip away, leaving behind thick yogurt cheese. Check occasionally to make sure the bottom of the strainer is not sitting in a pool of drained whey.

Using the side of a knife, smash the cardamom pods so that the peels loosen. With your fingers, pry out the seeds and use a mortar and pestle or a very clean spice grinder to grind them to a fine powder.

Heat the saffron threads in a small skillet over low heat until crisp, but be careful not to burn them. This should take less than 1 minute.

Place the yogurt cheese in a food processor. Add the sugar and pulse only until the sugar dissolves, 30 to 40 seconds. Do not overmix or the yogurt cheese will thin out too much. You do not want to whip the yogurt; shrikhand should be thick and creamy in consistency. For the perfect consistency, do what the Indians do—use a food mill with the finest disc attachment and pass the yogurt and sugar together through the mill at least 5 times to dissolve the sugar completely.

Crumble the toasted saffron over the shrikhand, fold in the pistachios and cardamom, and set aside, covered, for at least 2 hours for the flavors to blend. Serve cold or at room temperature. Shrikhand will last in the refrigerator, tightly covered in a glass dish, for 1 week.

Serves 4

rava tea cake with almond paste and rose water

Rava (cream of wheat) cakes are very popular in India. Baked in a range of vivid colors, they're served at teatime and often dipped in one's tea, a practice supposedly inherited from the British. My version adds almond paste and rose water to take this humble cake upmarket. I also like to serve it—dressed up with whipped cream and rose petals—as an elegant dessert.

½ cup (8 tablespoons) unsalted butter, softened

1 cup plus 1 tablespoon sugar, divided

1 cup coarse rava, *sooji*, or cream of wheat (not quick cooking)

4 ounces almond paste, cut into pieces (see Note)

2 tablespoons rose water

1 tablespoon brandy

4 large eggs, separated

¼ teaspoon cream of tartar

Sliced fresh fruit, such as bananas and strawberries

Confectioner's sugar for garnish

Whipped cream for garnish

Toasted slivered almonds for garnish

Preheat the oven to 350°F. Grease an 8-inch-square cake pan.

In the bowl of an electric mixer, cream the butter and 1 cup of the sugar until creamy. Add the rava, almond paste, rose water, and brandy, and continue beating until light and creamy. Beat in the egg yolks 1 at a time. After adding the last egg yolk, beat for an additional minute to develop structure.

In a clean, dry bowl, beat the egg whites until frothy. Add the cream of tartar, and beat until soft peaks form. While beating, slowly add the remaining 1 tablespoon sugar, and continue beating until the egg whites are stiff.

Add ¼ of the stiff egg whites to the cake batter, and fold in with swift strokes. This will lighten the mixture. Now add the rest of the egg whites and fold in gently yet firmly, without deflating the mixture. Scrape into the prepared cake pan, smooth the top, and bake in the center of the oven till golden brown all over and a cake tester inserted in the middle comes out clean, approximately 20 minutes.

To serve it up as a dessert, place some fresh fruit alongside each serving, dust with a little confectioner's sugar, and garnish with a dollop of freshly whipped cream and some toasted slivered almonds.

Serves **8**

NOTE: *You could also use marzipan, but remember that marzipan typically has more sugar in it than plain almond paste.*

cardamom nankaties

Nankaties (pronounced naan-kha-ties) are tiny cookies; they're one of the many traditional treats made by Indian Christians at Christmastime. The entire family is usually roped into the preparation, since each cookie needs to be individually hand rolled. Here's my version of this popular shortbread and, fortunately for you, I don't make them quite that small. Serve a platter of nankaties as an after-dinner treat, or stick a couple into a scoop of saffron ice cream.

¾ cup (12 tablespoons) unsalted butter, softened

1 cup confectioner's sugar

1¼ cups all-purpose flour

½ cup white rice flour (see Note, page 113)

¼ cup ground almonds

1 teaspoon ground cardamom

¼ teaspoon salt

Preheat the oven to 350°F.

In the bowl of an electric mixer, cream the butter and sugar until fluffy. Stir the flours, almonds, cardamom, and salt together, and add to the creamed butter. Mix just until the dough starts to clump together.

Using your hands, form the dough into a smooth ball. Pinch off a tablespoon-sized portion of the dough and roll in your palms to form a perfect round ball. Flatten it slightly and place on an ungreased baking sheet. Continue with the rest of the dough, placing the cookies on the sheet 2 inches apart. You can use a small ice cream scoop to measure out the cookie dough if you'd like.

Bake in the middle of the oven until the edges of the cookies turn a very pale brown, 15 to 18 minutes.

Cool on a wire rack, and store in an airtight container.

Makes approximately **30** cookies

creamy pumpkin kheer
with cashew nuts

My husband doesn't like sweets, and he likes pumpkin even less. But this dessert changed his mind. It's a sophisticated take on an everyday Indian pudding, or kheer, with the rice flour adding creaminess.

One small sugar pumpkin

2½ cups low-fat or whole milk

2 teaspoons rice flour (see Note, page 113)

1 tablespoon water

½ to ¾ cup sugar

6 to 8 whole green cardamom pods

12 raw cashews, chopped coarsely

¼ teaspoon finely grated nutmeg

Cut the pumpkin into wedges, then peel and seed it. Finely grate the pumpkin flesh until you have 2 cups. Wrap and refrigerate any leftover pumpkin for another use.

Using a steamer insert set over boiling water, steam the grated pumpkin until soft, about 10 minutes. Set aside.

Bring the milk to a boil in a large pan. Keep at a low boil until the milk thickens a little, about 10 minutes. Make a paste of the rice flour and water, and stir it into the thickened milk. Add the sugar and stir to dissolve. (Indians like their kheer sweet; add sugar to your taste here.)

Using the side of a knife, smash the cardamom pods so that the peels loosen. With your fingers, pry out the seeds and use a mortar and pestle or a very clean spice grinder to grind them to a fine powder.

Add the pumpkin, cashews, and cardamom to the milk and simmer an additional 5 minutes so the flavors meld. Stir in the nutmeg and remove from the heat.

Serve hot or cold.

Serves **4** to **6**

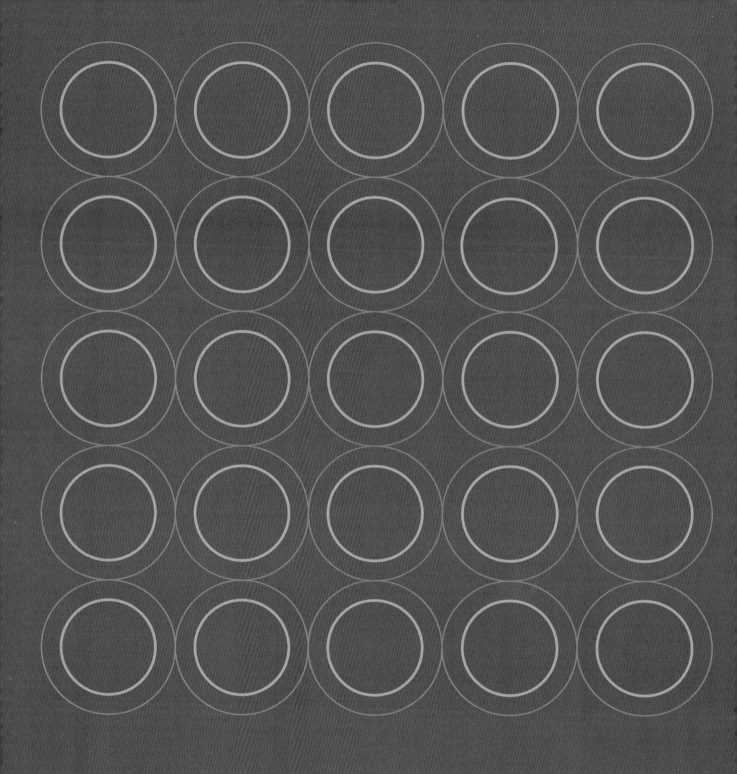

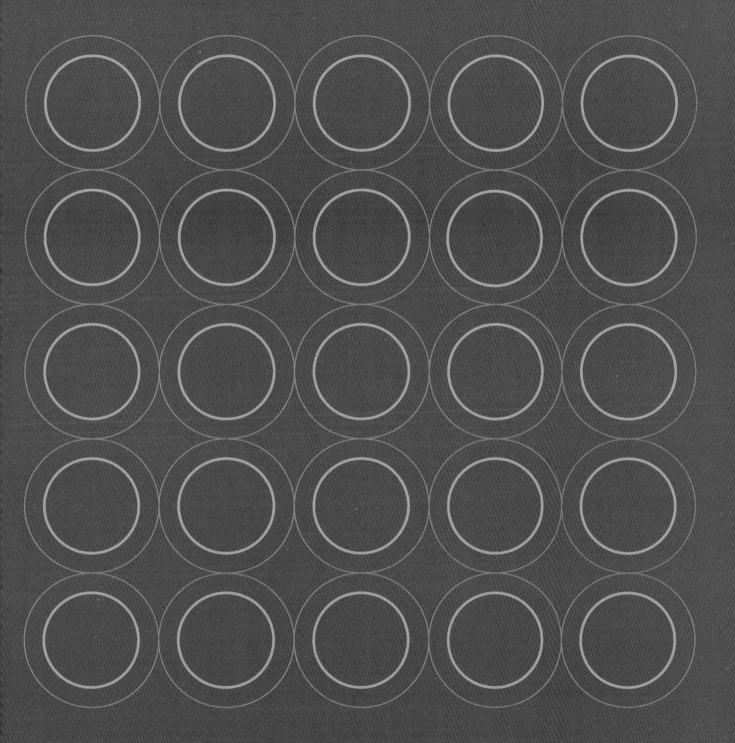

chapter **9:** a perfect cup of chai

Indians have an almost religious relationship with the creamy tea known as *chai*. No day can properly begin without a steaming cup of chai, whether you're sipping from fine bone china or a cheap clay cup. Your office will almost certainly have a designated "chai-boy" ferrying cups back and forth from the chai vendor across the street. After lunch comes another cup. Then there's teatime, around four o'clock, when you need a quick pick-me-up in the form of strong chai, served with a small savory snack. If you stop to visit a friend on the way home, chai will appear, and it's bad form to refuse. Your chai routine isn't interrupted even while traveling; whether you're in a car or on a train, a chai-boy will appear at your window before the vehicle has stopped moving.

Chai is essentially black tea brewed so strong that you have to add sugar and milk to reduce the tannins. Some people prefer it plain; others flavor it with a single ingredient like fresh ginger, or a special blend of spices called chai masala. Loose-leaf tea is always used, and the milk is always heated. And perhaps because people drink so much of it, chai is served in tiny glasses or small cups and saucers.

Here are some recipes for an exquisite cup of tea to jump-start your day or end an elegant dinner.

basic chai

The flavored chai recipes that follow are all based on this recipe. It's best to use loose-leaf tea, but a good brand of tea bag will also work. Choose a strong, black tea like English Breakfast, not a floral variety like Darjeeling.

1½ cups water

2 teaspoons sugar

2 heaped teaspoons loose-leaf black tea or 2 tea bags

½ cup low-fat or whole milk

Start with a clean saucepan with a lid; reserve this pan for making chai only. (This is to ensure that your tea doesn't accidentally taste of garlic.) Bring the water and sugar to a boil. Add the tea, let it boil for 2 seconds, and remove from the heat. Cover and steep until the tea leaves have settled to the bottom, from 3 to 5 minutes. Some teas are stronger than others and need less steeping time; you will have to experiment with your brand. Meanwhile, bring the milk to a boil. You may use the microwave; just remember it is essential that the milk be heated to boiling for best results.

Strain the tea into cups and add enough milk to make the tea a creamy orange color—about ¼ cup of milk per cup of chai. Serve immediately.

TIP: *Here's a trick I learned from my father, pour the hot milk into your cup of tea from a height of at least 6 inches; the froth makes a very attractive presentation.*

cardamom chai Using the flat side of a knife blade or the bottom of a small bowl, crush 2 cardamom pods. Add them—seeds, peel, and all—to the boiling water. Proceed with the Basic Chai recipe above.

vanilla bean chai Cut a 2-inch piece off a vanilla bean. Slice it in half lengthwise with a sharp paring knife. Add the bean—seeds and all—to the boiling water. Proceed with the Basic Chai recipe above.

lemongrass chai Bring 2 cups of water to a boil. Lightly bruise a 4-inch piece of fresh lemongrass with a kitchen mallet and add to the boiling water. Continue boiling until the total amount of water is reduced to 1½ cups, about 5 minutes. Proceed with the Basic Chai recipe above.

ginger chai Bring 2 cups of water to a boil. Rinse a 2-inch piece of fresh ginger, rubbing off any dirt or black spots with your fingers; you don't need to peel it. Lightly crush the ginger with a kitchen mallet and add to the boiling water. Continue boiling until the total amount of water is reduced to 1½ cups, about 5 minutes. Proceed with the Basic Chai recipe above.

Makes **2** cups

index

table of equivalents

The exact equivalents in the following tables have been rounded for convenience.

liquid/dry measures

U.S.	Metric
1/4 teaspoon	1.25 milliliters
1/2 teaspoon	2.5 milliliters
1 teaspoon	5 milliliters
1 tablespoon (3 teaspoons)	15 milliliters
1 fluid ounce (2 tablespoons)	30 milliliters
1/4 cup	60 milliliters
1/3 cup	80 milliliters
1/2 cup	120 milliliters
1 cup	240 milliliters
1 pint (2 cups)	480 milliliters
1 quart (4 cups, 32 ounces)	960 milliliters
1 gallon (4 quarts)	3.84 liters
1 ounce (by weight)	28 grams
1 pound	448 grams
2.2 pounds	1 kilogram

lengths

U.S.	Metric
1/8 inch	3 millimeters
1/4 inch	6 millimeters
1/2 inch	12 millimeters
1 inch	2.5 centimeters

oven temperatures

Fahrenheit	Celsius	Gas
250	120	1/2
275	140	1
300	150	2
325	160	3
350	180	4
375	190	5
400	200	6
425	220	7
450	230	8
475	240	9
500	260	10